# pasta

## EASY COOKING

STAR
FIRE

This is a Starfire book
First published in 2001

02 04 05 03

1 3 5 7 9 10 8 6 4 2

Starfire is part of
The Foundry Creative Media Company Limited
Crabtree Hall, Crabtree Lane, Fulham, London, SW6 6TY

Visit the Foundry website: www.foundry.co.uk/recipes

ISBN: 1-903817-01-3

The CIP record for this book is available from the British Library.

Printed in Italy


ACKNOWLEDGEMENTS

Authors: Catherine Atkinson, Juliet Barker, Liz Martin, Gina Steer,
Carol Tennant, Mari Mererid Williams and Elizabeth Wolf-Cohen
Editorial Consultant: Gina Steer
Project Editor: Karen Fitzpatrick
Photography: Colin Bowling, Paul Forrester and Stephen Brayne
Home Economists and Stylists: Jacqueline Bellefontaine,
Mandy Phipps, Vicki Smallwood and Penny Stephens
Design Team: Helen Courtney, Jennifer Bishop, Lucy Bradbury and Chris Herbert

All props supplied by Barbara Stewart at Surfaces

NOTE
Recipes using uncooked eggs should be avoided by infants,
the elderly, pregnant women and anyone suffering from an illness.

Special thanks to everyone involved in this book, particularly
Karen Fitzpatrick and Gina Steer.

# CONTENTS

## STARTERS

## FISH & SHELLFISH

# MEATS

# POULTRY & GAME

## VEGETABLES & SALADS

## ENTERTAINING

# Hygiene in the Kitchen

It is well worth remembering that many foods can carry some form of bacteria. In most cases, the worst it will lead to is a bout of food poisoning or gastroenteritis, although for certain groups this can be more serious – the risk can be reduced or eliminated by good food hygiene and proper cooking.

Do not buy food that is past its sell-by date and do not consume any food that is past its use-by date. When buying food, use the eyes and nose. If the food looks tired, limp or a bad colour or it has a rank, acrid or simply bad smell, do not buy or eat it under any circumstances.

Do take special care when preparing raw meat and fish. A separate chopping board should be used for each; wash the knife, board and the hands thoroughly before handling or preparing any other food.

Regularly clean, defrost and clear out the refrigerator or freezer – it is worth checking the packaging to see exactly how long each product is safe to freeze. Avoid handling food if suffering from an upset stomach as bacteria can be passed through food preparation.

Dish cloths and tea towels must be washed and changed regularly. Ideally use disposable cloths which should be replaced on a daily basis. More durable cloths should be left to soak in bleach, then washed in the washing machine on a boil wash.

Keep the hands, cooking utensils and food preparation surfaces clean and do not allow pets to climb on to any work surfaces.

## BUYING

Avoid bulk buying where possible, especially fresh produce such as meat, poultry, fish, fruit and vegetables unless buying for the freezer. Fresh foods lose their nutritional value rapidly so buying a little at a time minimises loss of nutrients. It also eliminates a packed refrigerator which reduces the effectiveness of the refrigeration process.

When buying prepackaged goods such as cans or pots of cream and yogurts, check that the packaging is intact and not damaged or pierced at all. Cans should not be dented, pierced or rusty. Check the sell-by dates even for cans and packets of dry ingredients such as flour and rice. Store fresh foods in the refrigerator as soon as possible – not in the car or the office.

When buying frozen foods, ensure that they are not heavily iced on the outside and the contents feel completely frozen. Ensure that the frozen foods have been stored in the cabinet at the correct storage level and the temperature is below 18°C/-0.4°F. Pack in cool bags to transport home and place in the freezer as soon as possible after purchase.

## PREPARATION

Make sure that all work surfaces and utensils are clean and dry. Hygiene should be given priority at all times. Separate chopping boards should be used for raw and cooked meats, fish and vegetables. Currently, a variety of good-quality plastic boards come in various designs and colours. This makes differentiating easier and the plastic has the added hygienic advantage of being washable at high temperatures in the dishwasher. (NB: If using the board for fish, first wash in cold water, then in hot to prevent odour!) Also, remember that knives and utensils should always be thoroughly cleaned after use.

When cooking, be particularly careful to keep cooked and raw food separate to avoid any contamination. It is worth washing all fruits and vegetables regardless of whether they are going to be eaten raw or lightly cooked. This rule should apply even to prewashed herbs and salads.

Do not reheat food more than once. If using a microwave, always check that the food is piping hot all the way through. (In theory, the food should reach 70°C/158°F and needs to be cooked at that temperature for at least three minutes to ensure that all bacteria are killed.)

All poultry must be thoroughly thawed before using, including chicken and poussin. Remove the food to be thawed from the freezer and place in a shallow dish to contain the juices. Leave the food in the refrigerator until it is completely thawed. A 1.4 kg/3 lb whole chicken will take about 26–30 hours to thaw. To speed up the process immerse the chicken in cold water. However, make sure that the water is changed regularly. When the joints can move freely and no ice crystals remain in the cavity, the bird is completely thawed.

Once thawed, remove the wrapper and pat the chicken dry. Place the chicken in a shallow dish, cover lightly and store as close to the base of the refrigerator as possible. The chicken should be cooked as soon as possible.

Some foods can be cooked from frozen including many prepacked foods such as soups, sauces, casseroles and breads. Where applicable follow the manufacturers' instructions.

Vegetables and fruits can also be cooked from frozen, but meats and fish should be thawed first. The only time food can be refrozen is when the food has been thoroughly thawed then cooked. Once the food has cooled then it can be frozen again. On such occasions the food can only be stored for one month.

All poultry and game (except for duck) must be cooked thoroughly. When cooked the juices will run clear from the thickest part of the bird – the best area to try is usually the thigh. Other meats, like minced meat and pork should be cooked right the way through. Fish should turn opaque, be firm in texture and break easily into large flakes.

When cooking leftovers, make sure they are reheated until piping hot and that any sauce or soup reaches boiling point first.

## STORING, REFRIGERATING AND FREEZING

Meat, poultry, fish, seafood and dairy products should all be refrigerated. The temperature of the refrigerator should be between 1–5°C/34–41°F while the freezer temperature should not rise above -18°C/-0.4°F.

To ensure the optimum refrigerator and freezer temperature, avoid leaving the door open for a long time. Try not to overstock the refrigerator as this reduces the airflow inside and affects the effectiveness in cooling the food within.

When refrigerating cooked food, allow it to cool down quickly and completely before refrigerating. Hot food will raise the temperature of the refrigerator and possibly affect or spoil other food stored in it.

Food within the refrigerator and freezer should always be covered. Raw and cooked food should be stored in separate parts of the refrigerator. Cooked food should be kept on the top shelves of the refrigerator, while raw meat, poultry and fish should be placed on bottom shelves to avoid drips and cross-contamination. It is recommended that eggs should be refrigerated in order to maintain their freshness and shelf life.

Take care that frozen foods are not stored in the freezer for too long. Blanched vegetables can be stored for one month; beef, lamb, poultry and pork for six months and unblanched vegetables and fruits in syrup for a year. Oily fish and sausages should be stored for three months. Dairy products can last four to six months while cakes and pastries should be kept in the freezer for three to six months.

## HIGH-RISK FOODS

Certain foods may carry risks to people who are considered vulnerable such as the elderly, the ill, pregnant women, babies, young infants and those suffering from a recurring illness.

It is advisable to avoid those foods listed below which belong to a higher-risk category.

There is a slight chance that some eggs carry the bacteria salmonella. Cook the eggs until both the yolk and the white are firm to eliminate this risk. Pay particular attention to dishes and products incorporating lightly cooked or raw eggs which should be eliminated from the diet.

Sauces including Hollandaise, mayonnaise, mousses, soufflés and meringues all use raw or lightly cooked eggs, as do custard-based dishes, ice creams and sorbets. These are all considered high-risk foods to the vulnerable groups mentioned above.

Certain meats and poultry also carry the potential risk of salmonella and so should be cooked thoroughly until the juices run clear and there is no pinkness left. Unpasteurised products such as milk, cheese (especially soft cheese), pâté, meat (both raw and cooked) all have the potential risk of listeria and should be avoided.

When buying seafood, buy from a reputable source which has a high turnover to ensure freshness. Fish should have bright clear eyes, shiny skin and bright pink or red gills. The fish should feel stiff to the touch, with a slight smell of sea air and iodine. The flesh of fish steaks and fillets should be translucent with no signs of discolouration.

Molluscs such as scallops, clams and mussels are sold fresh and are still alive. Avoid any that are open or do not close when tapped lightly. In the same way, univalves such as cockles or winkles should withdraw back into their shells when lightly prodded. When choosing cephalopods such as squid and octopus they should have a firm flesh and pleasant sea smell.

As with all fish, whether it is shellfish or seafish, care is required when freezing it. It is imperative to check whether the fish has been frozen before. If it has been frozen, then it should not be frozen again under any circumstances.

# How To Make Pasta

Home-made pasta has a light, almost silky texture and is very different from the fresh pasta that you can buy vacuum packed in supermarkets. It is also surprisingly easy to make and little equipment is needed; just a rolling pin and a sharp knife, although if you make pasta regularly it is worth investing in a pasta machine.

## MAKING BASIC EGG PASTA DOUGH

### Ingredients

*225 g/8 oz type 001 pasta flour, plus extra for dusting*
*1 tsp salt*
*2 eggs, plus 1 egg yolk*
*1 tbsp olive oil*
*1–3 tsp cold water*

*1* Sift the flour and salt into a mound on a clean work surface and make a well in the middle, keeping the sides quite high, so that the egg mixture will not trickle out when added.
*2* Beat together the eggs, yolk, oil and 1 teaspoon of water. Add to the well, then gradually work in the flour, adding extra water if needed, to make a soft but not sticky dough.
*3* Knead on a lightly floured surface for 5 minutes, or until the dough is smooth and elastic. Wrap in clingflim and leave to rest for 20 minutes at room temperature.

## USING A FOOD PROCESSOR

Sift the flour and salt into the bowl of a food processor fitted with a metal blade. Add the eggs, yolk, oil and water and pulse-blend until the ingredients are mixed and until the dough begins to come together, adding the extra water if needed. Knead for 1–2 minutes, then wrap and rest as before.

## ROLLING PASTA BY HAND

*1* Unwrap the pasta dough and cut in half. Work with just half at a time and keep the other half wrapped in clingfilm.
*2* Place the dough on a large, clean work surface lightly dusted with flour, then flatten with your hand and start to roll out. Always roll away from you, starting from the centre and giving the dough a quarter turn after each rolling. Sprinkle a little more flour over the dough if it starts to get sticky.
*3* Continue rolling and turning until the dough is as thin as possible; ideally about 3 mm/⅛ inch. Make sure that you roll it evenly, or some shapes will cook faster than others.

## ROLLING PASTA BY MACHINE

A machine makes smoother, thinner, more-even pasta than that made by hand-rolling. Most pasta machines work in the same way but you should refer to the manufacturers' instructions before using.

*1* Clamp the machine securely and attach the handle. Set the rollers at their widest setting and sprinkle lightly with flour. Cut the pasta into four pieces. Wrap 3 of them in clingfilm and reserve.
*2* Flatten the unwrapped pasta dough slightly, then feed it through the rollers. Fold the strip of dough in 3, rotate and feed through the rollers a second time. Continue to roll the pasta this way, narrowing the roller setting by one notch every second time and flouring the rollers if the pasta starts to get sticky. Only fold the dough the first time it goes through each roller width. The dough will get longer and thinner with every rolling – if it gets too difficult to handle, cut the strip in half and work with 1 piece at a time.
*3* If making spaghetti or noodles such as tagliatelle, the second last setting is

generally used. For pasta shapes and filled pastas, the dough should be rolled to the finest setting.
*4* Fresh pasta should be dried slightly before cutting. Either drape over a narrow wooden pole for 5 minutes or place on a clean tea towel sprinkled with a little flour for 10 minutes.

You can also buy electric pasta machines that carry out the whole pasta-making process, from dough mixing and kneading, to extruding it through cutters into the required shapes – all you have to do is weigh out and add the individual ingredients. They can make over 900 g/ 2 lb of pasta at a time, but are expensive to buy and take up a lot of space.

## SHAPING UP

When cutting and shaping freshly made pasta, have 2 or 3 lightly floured tea-towels ready. Arrange the pasta in a single layer, spaced slightly apart, or you may find that they stick together. When they are dry, you can freeze them successfully for up to 6 weeks, by layering in suitable freezer containers between sheets of baking parchment. Spread them out on baking parchment for about 20 minutes, or slightly longer if stuffed, before cooking. When making pasta, do not throw away the trimmings. They can be cut into tiny shapes or thin slivers and used in soups.

*Farfalle* Use a fluted pasta wheel to cut the pasta sheets into rectangles about 2.5 x 5 cm/1 x 12 inches. Pinch the long sides of each rectangle in the middle to make a bow. Spread out on a floured tea towel and leave to dry for at least 15 minutes.

*Lasagne* This is one of the easiest to make. Simply trim the pasta sheets until neat and cut into lengths the same size as your lasagne dish. Spread the cut sheets on tea towels sprinkled with flour.

*Macaroni* This is the generic name for hollow pasta. Cut the rolled-out pasta dough into squares, then wrap each around a chopstick, thick skewer or similar, starting from one of the corners. Slip the pasta off, curve slightly if liked and leave to dry for at least 15 minutes.

*Noodles* If using a pasta machine, use the cutter attachment to produce tagliatelle or fettucine, or use a narrower one for tagliarini or spaghetti. To make by hand, sprinkle the rolled-out pasta with flour, then roll up like a Swiss roll and cut into thin slices. The thickness of these depends on the noodles required. For linguine, cut into 5 mm/¼ inch slices and for tagliatelle cut into 8 mm/⅓ inch slices. Unravel them immediately after cutting. To make thicker ribbon pasta such as pappardelle, use a serrated pastry wheel to cut into wide strips. Leave over a wooden pole for up to 5 minutes to dry out.

*Ravioli* Cut the rolled-out sheet of dough in half widthways. Cover one half with clingfilm to stop it drying out too quickly. Brush the other sheet of dough with beaten egg. Pipe or spoon small mounds – using about 1 teaspoon of filling in even rows, spacing them at 4 cm/1½ inch intervals. Remove the clingfilm from the reserved pasta sheet and using a rolling pin carefully lift over the dough with the filling. Press down firmly between the pockets of filling to push out any air. Finally, cut into squares with a pastry cutter or sharp knife. Leave on a floured tea towel for 45 minutes before cooking.

You can also use a ravioli tray (*raviolatore*) to produce perfect even-sized ravioli. A sheet of rolled-out dough is laid over the tray, then pressed into the individual compartments. The filling can then be spooned or piped into the indentations and the second sheet of dough placed on top. To create the individual ravioli squares, a rolling pin is gently rolled over the serrated top. These tins are excellent for making small ravioli containing a little filling.

Three or four simple ingredients combined together make the best fillings. Always season generously with salt and freshly ground black pepper and where the filling is soft, stir in a little beaten egg. Why not try chopped cooked spinach, ricotta and freshly grated nutmeg; finely ground turkey, curd cheese, tarragon and Parmesan cheese; white crabmeat with mascarpone, finely grated lemon rind and dill; or ricotta, roasted garlic and fresh herbs.

*Silhouette Pasta* If rolled out very thinly, fresh herb leaves can be sandwiched between 2 layers of pasta for a stunning silhouette effect. Put the pasta through a machine set on the very last setting, so that it is paper-thin. Cut in half and lightly brush 1 piece with water. Arrange individual fresh herb leaves at regular intervals over the moistened pasta (you will need soft herbs for this – flat-leaf parsley, basil and sage are all ideal). Place the second sheet of dry pasta on top and gently press with a rolling pin to seal them together. Sprinkle the pasta with a little flour, then put it through the machine on the second to finest setting. Use a pastry wheel, dipped in flour, to cut around the herb leaves to make squares, or use a round or oval cutter to stamp out the pasta if preferred. Leave to dry on a floured tea towel for 20 minutes before cooking.

*Tortellini* Use a plain biscuit cutter to stamp out rounds of pasta about 5 cm/2 inches in diameter. Lightly brush each with beaten egg, then spoon or pipe about 1 teaspoon of filling into the middle of each round. Fold in half to make a half-moon shape, gently pressing the edges together to seal. Bend the 2 corners round and press together to seal. Allow to dry on a floured tea towel for 30 minutes before cooking. To make tortelloni, use a slightly larger cutter; about 6.5 cm/2½ inches.

*Variations*

Flavoured pastas are simple and there are dozens of delicious ways that you can change the flavour and colour of pasta. You will find that you get a more-even colour when using a machine, but the speckled appearance of flavoured hand-rolled pasta can be equally attractive.

*Chilli* Add 2 teaspoons of crushed, dried red chillies to the egg mixture before you mix with the flour.

*Herb* Stir 3 tablespoons of chopped fresh herbs such as basil, parsley, marjoram or sage or 2 tablespoons of finely chopped, strongly-flavoured herbs like thyme or rosemary into the flour.

*Olive* Blend 2 tablespoons of black olive paste with the egg mixture, leaving out the water.

*Porcini* Soak 15 g/½ oz dried porcini mushrooms in boiling water for 20 minutes. Drain and squeeze out as much water as possible, then chop very finely. Add to the egg mixture. (Reserve the soaking liquor, strain and use to flavour the pasta sauce.)

*Saffron* Sift 1 teaspoon of powdered saffron with the flour.

*Spinach* Cook 75 g/3 oz prepared spinach in a covered pan with just the water clinging to the leaves, until wilted. Drain and squeeze dry, then chop finely. Add to the egg mixture.

*Sun-dried Tomato* Blend 2 tablespoons of sun-dried tomato paste into the egg mixture, leaving out the water.

*Wholemeal Pasta* Substitute half the wholemeal flour for half of the white flour and add an extra 1–2 teaspoons water to the mixture.

# Pasta Varieties

Pasta has been twisted and curled into an unimaginable number of shapes. There is a vast range of both fresh and dried pasta; short and long, tiny varieties for soup, larger ones for stuffing and more unusual designer shapes and flavours.

## DRIED PASTAS

*Buckwheat Pasta* Darker in colour than wholewheat pasta, this is made from buckwheat flour. It is gluten-free so is suitable for people who are intolerant to wheat products. Pizzoccheri are thin, flat noodles twisted into nests and are the most common type of buckwheat pasta.

*Corn Pasta* Now found on most supermarket shelves, corn pasta is made with maize flour and the plain variety is a bright yellow colour. Like buckwheat pasta, it is gluten-free. When cooking, make sure you use a large saucepan as it tends to cause the water to foam more than ordinary wheat pasta.

*Coloured and Flavoured Pasta* The varieties of these types of pasta are endless. The most popular and easily obtainable are spinach and tomato. Often three colours (white, red and green) are packed together and labelled 'tricolore'. Others available in larger food stores and delicatessens include beetroot, saffron, herb, poppy seed, garlic, chilli, mushroom, smoked saffron and black ink. More unusual types such as blue curaco liqueur pasta, which has a bright turquoise colour, have also been created.

*Durum Wheat Pasta* This is the most readily available and may be made with or without eggs. Generally plain wheat pasta is used for long, straight shapes such as spaghetti, whereas pasta containing eggs is slightly more fragile, so is packed into nests or waves. Look for the words 'Durum wheat' or '*pasta di semola di grano duro*' on the packet when buying, as pastas made from soft wheat tend to become soggy when cooked.

*Wholewheat Pasta* Made with wholemeal flour, this has a higher fibre content than ordinary pasta which gives it a slightly chewy texture, nutty flavour and rich brown colour. Wholewheat pasta takes longer to cook, however, than the refined version. We tend to think of it as a modern product associated with the growth in interest of health foods, but it has been made in north-eastern Italy for hundreds of years, where it is known as *bigoli* and is like a thick spaghetti.

## PASTA SHAPES
### Long Pasta
*Spaghetti* Probably the best known type of pasta, spaghetti derives its name from the word *spago* meaning string, which describes its round, thin shape perfectly. Spaghettini is a thinner variety and spaghettoni is thicker. Vermicelli is a very fine type of spaghetti.

*Tagliatelle* Tagliatelle is the most common type of ribbon-noodle pasta and each ribbon of pasta is usually slightly less than 1 cm/½ inch wide. It is traditionally from Bologna where it always accompanies bolognaise sauce (rather than spaghetti). It is sold coiled into nests that unravel when cooked. Thinner varieties of tagliarini or tagliolini are also available. A mixture of white and spinach-flavoured tagliatelle

is known as *paglia e fieno* which translates as straw and hay. Fettucine is the Roman version of tagliatelle and is cut slightly thinner.

*Ziti* Long, thick and hollow, ziti may be ridged but is usually smooth. It takes its name from *zita*, meaning fiancee, as it was once traditional to serve it at weddings in southern Italy. Zitoni is a similar larger pasta; mezza zita is thinner.

### Short Pasta
There are basically two types of short pasta: *secca* is factory-made from durum wheat and water, which is pressed into assorted shapes and sizes, and *pasta all'uovo* is made with eggs, which is particularly popular in northern Italy, where it is served with meat or creamy sauces. *Pasta all'uovo* is slightly more expensive than plain pasta, but cooks in less time and is less likely to go soggy if overcooked. It is also much more nutritious and has an attractive golden colour. There are hundreds of different shapes and some of the most popular ones are listed below.

*Conchiglie* As the name implies, these pasta shapes resemble conch shells and are ideal for serving with thinner sauces which will get trapped in the shells. Sizes vary from very tiny ones to large ones which are suitable for stuffing. They may be smooth or ridged conchiglie rigate.

*Eliche and Fusilli* These are twisted into the shape of a screw, which is where their name comes from. Eliche is often wrongly labelled as fusilli as the two are similar, but fusilli is more tightly coiled and opens out slightly during cooking.

*Farfalle* A popular pasta shape, these are bow or butterfly shaped, often with crinkled edges.

*Gnocchi Sardi* These come from Sardinia and are named after the little gnocchi potato dumplings. Often served with rich meat sauces, they have a somewhat chewy texture.

*Macaroni* This is known as maccheroni in Italy. You may find it labelled as 'elbow macaroni' which describes its shape (although it is sometimes almost straight). This was once the most popular imported pasta and is particularly good in baked dishes, notably macaroni cheese. A thin, quick-cook variety is also available.

*Penne* Slightly larger, hollow tubes than macaroni, the ends are cut diagonally and are pointed like quills. There are also less well-known varieties including the thinner pennette and even thinner pennini. They are often made with egg or flavoured with tomato or spinach.

*Pipe* This is curved, hollow pasta and is often sold ridged as pipe rigate. The smaller type is known as pipette.

*Rigatoni* This is substantial, chunky, tubular pasta and is often used for baking. Because the pasta is thick, it tends to be slightly chewier than other short pastas. Rigatoni goes well with meat and strongly flavoured sauces.

*Rotelle* This is thin, wheel-shaped pasta, also known as ruote and trulli and often sold in packets of two or three colours.

## FLAT PASTA

There are many types of long, flat ribbon pastas, but there is only one flat pasta – lasagne – which is usually used for baking in the oven (al forno). These thin sheets are layered up with a sauce or may be curled into large tubes about 10 cm/4 inches long to make cannelloni. In Italy, they are usually made from fresh sheets of lasagne rolled around the filling, however, dried tubes are easily available and simple to use.

Three flavours of lasagne are available: plain, spinach or wholewheat. Most sheets are flat, but some have curled edges which help trap the sauce during cooking and stop it running to the bottom of the dish. Lasagnette are long, narrow strips of flat pasta and are crimped on one or both long edges. Like lasagne, they are designed to be layered up with a sauce and baked.

## STUFFED PASTA

Tortellini are the most common of dried pasta shapes and consist of tiny, stuffed pieces of pasta which are folded, and then the ends are joined to make a ring. A speciality of Bologna, larger ones are made from rounds or squares and are joined without leaving a hole in the middle. They are called tortelloni and generally are made with a meat (*alla carne*) or cheese (*ai formaggi*) filling and will keep for up to a year (but always check the sell-by date). Cappelletti, ravioli and agnalotti are sometimes sold dried, but more often fresh.

## SOUP PASTA

Tiny pasta shapes known as *pastina* in Italy come in hundreds of different shapes and are often added to soups. Risi is the smallest type of pasta and looks like grains of rice, whereas orzi, another soup pasta, resembles barley. Slightly larger ones include, stellette (stars), and rotelli (wheels). Many are miniature shapes of larger pasta; farfallette (little bows) and conchigliette (little shells).

## FRESH PASTA

Fresh pasta has become increasingly popular over the past decade and can be found in the chilled cabinets of supermarkets, as well as being sold loose in specialist shops. Ideally, you should buy fresh pasta on the day you are going to cook it, or use within a day or two. It must be stored in the refrigerator until you are ready to use it, as it contains eggs, which shorten its

keeping time. It is generally available in the same shapes as dried pasta, but has a much greater range of stuffed fillings. Ravioli is one of the most common. It is shaped into large squares with fluted edges and is made with many different pasta doughs including saffron and fresh herbs. The fillings may be anything, for example, spinach and ricotta, mushroom, fish and shellfish, meat, but especially chicken. They may also be shaped into long rectangles, circles or ovals.

## ORIENTAL NOODLES

Pasta originated in China and not in Italy, so it is hardly surprising that there is a vast range of oriental noodles.

*Buckwheat Noodles* Soba are the most common and are a dark, greyish-brown colour. They feature in Japanese cooking in soups and stir-fries.

*Cellophane Noodles* Made from mung beans, these are translucent, flavourless noodles and are only available dried. They are never boiled and simply need soaking in very hot water.

*Egg Noodles* Commonly used in Chinese cooking, they come in several thicknesses; thin and medium being the most popular.

*Rice Noodles* These are fine, delicate, opaque noodles which are made from rice and are often used in Thai and Malaysian cooking.

*Urdon Noodles* These are thick Japanese noodles which can be round or flat and are available both fresh, dried or precooked.

# Pasta Techniques and Tips

## STEPS TO COOKING PERFECT PASTA

Follow a few simple rules to ensure that your pasta is cooked to perfection every time:

1 Choose a big saucepan – there needs to be plenty of room for the pasta to move around during cooking so that it does not stick together. The most convenient type of saucepan has a built-in perforated inner pan, so that the pasta can be lifted out of the water and drained as soon as it is cooked.
2 Cook the pasta in a large quantity of fast-boiling, well-salted water; ideally about 4 litres/7 pints of water and 1½–2 tablespoons of salt for every 350 g/ 12 oz–450 g/1 lb of pasta. Some cooks say that the addition of 1–2 teaspoons of olive or sunflower oil not only helps to stop the water boiling over but also helps to prevent the pasta from sticking. However, other cooks believe that as long as the saucepan is large enough and the water is on a full-rolling boil, the pasta will not stick together nor will the water boil over.
3 Tip in the pasta all at once, give it a stir and cover with a lid. Quickly bring back to a rolling boil then remove the lid – do not cover with a lid during cooking. Once it is boiling, turn down the heat to medium-high and cook the pasta for the required time. It should be 'al dente' which literally translates as 'to the tooth' and means that the pasta should be tender, but still firm to the bite. Test frequently towards the end of cooking time; the only way to do this is to take out a piece and try it. Stir the pasta occasionally during cooking with a wooden spoon or fork to make sure that it does not stick to the pan.
4 As soon as the pasta is ready, drain in a colander (or by lifting the draining pan up and out of the water if you have a pasta pot with an inner drainer). Give it a shake, so that any trapped water can drain

out. At this stage you can toss the pasta in a little oil or butter if you are not mixing it with a sauce. Reserve a little of the cooking water to stir into the pasta, this not only helps to thin the sauce if necessary, but also helps prevent the cooked pasta sticking together as it cools.

Some pastas need a little more care when cooking than others. Never stir stuffed pastas vigorously, or they may split open and the filling will be lost in the cooking water. When cooking long, dried pasta such as spaghetti, you will need to coil the pasta into the water as it starts to soften. Hold one end of the strands of spaghetti and push the other to the bottom of the pan, coiling them round, and using a wooden spoon or fork, when the boiling water gets too close to your hand.

An alternative cooking method is to add the pasta to boiling salted water as before, then boil rapidly for 2 minutes. Cover the pan with a tight-fitting lid and turn off the heat. Leave to stand for the full cooking time, then drain and serve in the usual way. Pasta may also be cooked successfully in a microwave, although it does not cook any faster than on the hob. Put the pasta in a large bowl, add salt, then pour over enough boiling water to cover the pasta by at least 2.5 cm/1 inch. Microwave on High (100% power) for the times given below. Allow the pasta to stand for 2–3 minutes before draining.

## PASTA COOKING TIMES

Start timing from the moment that the pasta returns to the boil; not from when it was added. Use a kitchen timer if possible, as even a few seconds too long may spoil the pasta.

*Fresh* 2–3 minutes for thin noodles (although very fine pastas may be ready within seconds of the pasta boiling), thick noodles and shapes 3–4 minutes and filled pastas 5–7 minutes.

*Dried* 8–12 minutes; filled pastas can take up to 20 minutes to cook, however, you should always check the packet instructions, as some pastas labelled 'quick cook' only take about 4 minutes.

## SERVING QUANTITIES

As an approximate guide, allow 75–125 g (3–4 oz) uncooked pasta per person. Obviously the amount will depend on whether the pasta is being served for a light or main meal and the type of sauce that it is being served with.

## MATCHING PASTA TYPES AND SAUCES

It is entirely up to you which pasta you serve with which sauce but in general, heavier sauces with large chunks of meat or vegetables go less with pastas that will trap the sauce and meat in curls and hollows, such as penne, shells, riagatoni or spirals. On the other hand, soft fluid sauces suit long pastas such as linguine, pappardelle, or tagliatelle.

### Classic Sauces

*Alla Carbonara* Pasta with ham, eggs and cream – the heat of the pasta cooks the eggs to thicken the sauce.

*Alla Napoletana* Made from fresh tomatoes, but with olive oil, garlic and onions.

*All'arrabiata* A hot sauce with red chillies, tomatoes and chopped bacon.

*All'aglio e Olio* Pasta with olive oil and finely chopped garlic.

*Alla Marinara* A fresh tomato and basil sauce, sometimes with wine (not seafood).

*Con Ragù* Meat sauce from Bologna (known as bolognaise sauce in English), often made with half minced pork and half minced beef. This is traditionally served with tagliatelle and not spaghetti.

## SERVING PASTA

In Italy, pasta is usually dressed with the sauce before serving to combine the flavours, but you can top the pasta with the sauce if you prefer, in which case, toss it in a little olive oil or butter to give it an attractive sheen. Cook the sauce and pasta so that they will both be ready at the same time; most sauces can be left to stand for a few minutes and reheated when the pasta is ready. If the pasta is ready before the sauce, drain it, and return to the pan with a tight-fitting lid – it should be fine for a few minutes. Always serve in warmed serving bowls or plates, as pasta loses heat very quickly.

## SERVING WINES WITH PASTA

If possible, choose a wine that comes from the same region as the dish you are serving. If there is wine in the sauce, you will be able to serve the rest of the bottle with your meal, so make sure you choose one that you enjoy drinking. Otherwise, pick a wine that matches the strongest-flavoured ingredient in the sauce. Rich, meaty sauces or highly spiced ones with lots of garlic need a robust, full-bodied wine to go with them. Of course, there is no reason why you should stick to Italian wines and if you are serving an oriental pasta dish you may opt for lager or other drinks. Below are ten well-known types of Italian wine.

### White Wines

*Chardonnay* This wine is produced in many parts of the world and is wonderful served with fish dishes. The Italian chardonnay has a faint lemony flavour.

*Frascati* This wine is made near Rome and is one of the most popular Italian wines. It is crisp and fruity and has quite a lot of body. It goes well with most foods.

*Orvieto* This wine is named after the town of the same name, just north of Rome. It is dry and soft with a slightly nutty and fruity flavour and is good for summer drinking and serving with fish and white meats.

*Soave* This wine is one of Italy's most famous wines. The best ones have a distinct hint of almonds and are dry and crisp. It goes well with shellfish, chicken and light vegetable pasta sauces.

*Verdiccho* This wine comes in a carved amphora bottle and in Italy is known as *La Lollobrigida*. A crisp, clean and dry white wine with a slightly metallic edge, it is best when served with fish and seafood.

### Red Wines

*Barbaresco* This wine is full-bodied with an intense flavour and a high tannin content. It teams well with rich pasta dishes, especially beef.

*Bardolino* This is light and fruity with an almost cherry and slightly bitter almond taste; perfect for duck and game.

*Barolo* This is one of Italy's finest wines and is a full-bodied red. Serve with rich meaty dishes, game or spicy sausage pasta sauces.

*Chianti* This wine is best drunk when young and may be served slightly chilled. It is often regarded as the classic accompaniment to pasta.

## PASTA EQUIPMENT

When making and cooking pasta, a bare minimum of equipment is needed; some would say that a rolling pin, a large pan and a colander would suffice, however, there are many gadgets that make the process a lot easier.

### When Making

*Rolling Pin* Try to use one that is quite slender and choose a conventional wooden one without handles. In Italy pasta rolling pins are very long, for rolling out large quantities of pasta at a time, and slightly thicker in the middle with tapering ends.

*Pasta Machine* A traditional, hand-cranked pasta machine has adjusting rollers and usually cutters for making tagliatelle and finer tagliarini. More complicated ones come with a selection of cutters.

*Pasta Wheel* This is useful for cutting noodles such as tagliatelle and pappardelle if you do not have a pasta machine and also for stuffed shapes such as ravioli. This is an inexpensive piece of equipment and less likely to drag or tear the pasta than a knife.

*Ravioli Cutter* Specially designed, fluted-edged cutters can be bought for cutting pasta. A fluted or plain biscuit cutter works just as well.

### When Cooking and Serving

*Long-handled Pasta Fork* This is useful for stirring the pasta to keep the pieces separate during cooking. You can also get wooden pasta hooks which will lift out the strands of pasta so that you can check whether or not it is cooked.

*Parmesan Graters* These range from simple hand graters to electrical gadgets. If sharp, the fine side of a box grater works equally well.

*Parmesan Knife* This is used to shave Parmesan off a block. A vegetable peeler may be used as an alternative.

*Pasta Cooking Pot* Officially this should be tall with straight sides and handles and should have an inner basket. When buying, choose one that is not too heavy, and will be easy to manage when full.

*Pasta Measurer* This is a wooden gadget with several holes for measuring spaghetti. Each hole takes a different amount of pasta for a given number of people.

# Pasta Pantry

## INGREDIENTS FOR MAKING EGG PASTA

Only four simple ingredients are needed for basic pasta dough: flour, eggs, olive oil and salt.

*Eggs* These should be as fresh as possible and preferably free-range which tend to have deeper-coloured yolks, and therefore, give the pasta a richer, more golden colour. They should be kept at room temperature and not used straight from the refrigerator when making pasta.

*Flour* The best flour for pasta is Farina Bianca 00 or Tipo 00 and can be bought from Italian food stores. This type of flour is a very fine wheat flour imported from Italy. You can use strong, white bread flour as an alternative, but the dough will be more difficult to roll out, especially if you are making the pasta by hand.

*Olive Oil* Strictly speaking, this is not essential for pasta but it gives the dough flavour and makes it slightly softer and therefore easier to roll. Olive oil varies in flavour and colour, depending on where it comes from. Generally, those from hotter climates such as southern Italy and Spain have a stronger flavour and darker colour than those from areas such as as France. Pure or light olive oil is refined to remove any impurities, is

then blended and has a light flavour. Virgin olive oil is a pure first-pressed oil, and extra-virgin is a superior product which comes from the first cold pressing of the olives and must have a low acidity; less than 1 per cent.

*Salt* Vital for flavour and should be finely ground, whether ordinary or sea salt.

## INGREDIENTS FOR PASTA SAUCES

*Anchovies* These are small, silvery fish that grow up to 10 cm/4 inches long and for centuries have been preserved in salt. They are generally bought as fillets in small cans of around 50 g/ 2 oz. When chopped and mixed with olive oil and garlic, they make an excellent, simple pasta sauce. They are very salty, so bear this in mind when adding seasoning, or if other salty ingredients are being used. Anchovies should be soaked in a little milk or water for about 20 minutes before using.

*Capers* These are the green flower buds of a bush that grows around the shores of the Mediterranean and they add a sharp piquancy to sauces. Most are sold bottled in vinegar which makes them particularly good with fish and seafood. If you buy salted capers, rinse them thoroughly, then soak for a few minutes to remove excess salt.

*Cheeses* Many cheeses feature in pasta dishes, but you do not have to stick to Italian varieties. However, these naturally go well with Italian-flavoured pasta dishes. Gorgonzola is a blue-veined cheese from Lombardy. It melts quickly, so is good in sauces and is also used for stuffing pastas such as ravioli. Mascarpone is a rich, fresh creamy cheese that melts without curdling. It can be added to pasta with fresh herbs

to make a quick sauce. Parmesan is often grated over pasta dishes or shaved into paper-thin curls when serving. Ricotta is a fresh, soft white cheese that melts beautifully. It has a somewhat bland taste, so is most often combined with other ingredients, such as fresh herbs.

*Herbs* Both fresh and dried herbs enhance pasta dishes. Those most frequently used are basil, bay leaves, coriander, dill, oregano and marjoram, parsley, rosemary and thyme. Basil has a natural affinity with tomatoes and its sweet, fragrant flavour counteracts any acidity. Although basil originated in India, the Italians grow it prolifically. It should be torn or shredded and added at the last moment so that it retains its bright green colour and pungent flavour. Dried basil is a poor substitute for fresh – it is better to add a spoonful of green pesto. Look out for a recent addition, purple-coloured basil, which looks especially attractive when used as a garnish on simple dishes such as pasta tossed in olive oil, garlic and cheese

Bay Leaves are often used to flavour white sauces and meat dishes such as bolognaise. They are always removed before serving, although fresh ones make an attractive garnish. Coriander is rarely used in Italian pasta dishes, but is often used in oriental noodle dishes. Dill, with its feathery leaves and aniseed flavour, is used a lot in fish and seafood dishes. Oregano and marjoram are frequently used with tomatoes. Oregano is the wild strain and has a less delicate flavour than marjoram, although the two are interchangeable in dishes.

Recently, curly-leafed parsley has been upstaged by flat-leaf, also known as Italian or Continental parsley, although either can be used. Rosemary is probably the most pungent herb available and should be used sparingly. Either remove the leaves from the sprig or add the whole sprig to sauces, then remove at the end of cooking and discard.

Thyme is a strongly flavoured herb and although it is better fresh, dried makes a reasonable substitute. It goes well in meat and strongly flavoured dishes. Always strip the leaves off the woody stem before chopping.

*Mushrooms* There are many varieties of fresh, cultivated and wild mushrooms that feature in pasta sauces. Dried porcini mushrooms are also often used for their intense flavour. Only a very small amount is needed; 10-15 g/½ oz is enough for a dish to serve four people. Always soak them first in warm water, then strain the soaking liquid to remove any grit and add to the sauce as well as the mushrooms.

*Olives* Both black and green olives are used in sauces. Sometimes they are chopped, but more often are used whole (but make sure you stone them first). Buy plain ones in olive oil for adding to sauces; the small shiny ones have the best flavour and should be added at the end of cooking time, or they may become slightly bitter.

*Pesto* The best pesto is most definetly homemade – there is no substitute. Blend fresh basil leaves with olive oil, pine nuts and freshly grated Parmesan cheese. Some supermarkets, however, sell fresh pesto in tubs in the chilled cabinet. The bottled varieties come as green and red (which is made from sun-dried tomatoes and red peppers). Pesto adds richness and flavour to sauces, or may be used on its own, simply tossed with cooked pasta.

*Pine Nuts* A vital ingredient of pesto, these small, creamy white nuts have a buttery texture and a hint of pine resin. Buy in small quantities and store in the refrigerator.

*Spices* Spices are often added to pasta dishes, most notably to those made with Eastern noodles. They include chillies, garlic and saffron. Small red chillies are popular in pasta dishes from southern Italy, but are usually added in small quantities to enhance flavour, rather than to make them hot and fiery. Garlic should be used in small quantities to enhance flavour. The combination of olive oil and garlic forms the basis of many pasta sauces. The longer garlic is cooked the more mellow the flavour. When buying, look for heads which are firm and showing no signs of sprouting; larger cloves have a sweeter flavour. Saffron is the world's most expensive spice. The stigmas are gathered from the saffron crocus and just a pinch will add a rich, golden colour and fragrant flavour to your dish – a little saffron goes a long way.

*Tomatoes* Many tomato products come from southern Italy where they are ripened on the vine in the hot sun. It is hardly surprising that they feature in so many pasta dishes. The simplest of sauces can be made from canned, peeled plum tomatoes which come whole or chopped and can now be bought with added flavourings such as chilli, basil and peppers. These are excellent when fresh tomatoes are not at their best flavour-wise.

Passata is pulped tomatoes that have been strained to remove the seeds. It comes in cartons and is a useful addition to the storecupboard. Sun-dried tomatoes may be plain, dried or in oil. The dried variety needs re-hydrating. This can be done by chopping the sun-dried tomatoes and adding them to a sauce that needs to be cooked for a long time. If you are making a quick sauce, then soften the sun-dried tomatoes by soaking them in hot water for a couple of hours before using. Sun-dried tomatoes in oil already have a soft texture and are excellent for adding a deep, almost roasted flavour to pasta dishes.

*Tomato Purée* This is a strong, thick paste made from tomatoes, salt and citric acid. It is sold in tubes and jars – only a little is needed to give your dish a rich, tomato taste. Too much tomato purée can overpower a dish and make it acidic. Sun-dried tomato purée has a sweeter and milder flavour and is a thick mixture of sun-dried tomatoes and olive oil.

*Vinegar* A dash of red or white wine vinegar may be added to a pasta dish, but the most frequently used in modern cooking is balsamic vinegar (a rich, sweetish, smooth brown vinegar aged in wooden barrels until the flavour is very mellow). The best balsamic vinegars are matured for 40 years upwards and are therefore very expensive. Cheaper ones sold in supermarkets have been aged for four to five years and are perfect for adding to sauces.

# Fresh Tagliatelle with Courgettes

**1** Sift the flour and salt into a large bowl, make a well in the centre and add the eggs and yolk, 1 tablespoon of oil with 1 teaspoon of water. Gradually mix to form a soft but not sticky dough, adding a little more flour or water as necessary. Turn out on to a lightly floured surface and knead for 5 minutes, or until smooth and elastic. Wrap in clingfilm and leave to rest at room temperature for about 30 minutes.

**2** Divide the dough into 8 pieces. Feed a piece of dough through a pasta machine. Gradually decrease the settings on the rollers, feeding the pasta through each time, until the sheet is very long and thin. If the pasta seems sticky, dust the work surface and both sides of the pasta generously with flour. Cut in half crosswise and hang over a clean pole. Repeat with the remaining dough. Leave to dry for about 5 minutes. Feed each sheet through the tagliatelle cutter, hanging the cut pasta over the pole. Leave to dry for a further 5 minutes. Wind a handful of pasta strands into nests and leave on a floured tea towel. Repeat with the remaining dough and leave to dry for 5 minutes.

**3** Cook the pasta in plenty of salted boiling water for 2–3 minutes, or until 'al dente'.

**4** Meanwhile, heat the remaining oil in a large frying pan and add the courgettes, garlic, chilli and lemon zest. Cook over a medium heat for 3–4 minutes, or until the courgettes are lightly golden and tender.

**5** Drain the pasta thoroughly, reserving 2 tablespoons of the cooking water. Add the pasta to the courgettes with the basil and seasoning. Mix well, adding the reserved cooking water. Serve with the Parmesan cheese.

## INGREDIENTS
### Serves 4–6

*225 g /8 oz strong plain bread flour or type 00 pasta flour, plus extra for rolling*
*1 tsp salt*
*2 medium eggs*
*1 medium egg yolk*
*3 tbsp extra virgin olive oil*
*2 small courgettes, halved lengthwise and thinly sliced*
*2 garlic cloves, peeled and thinly sliced*
*large pinch chilli flakes*
*zest of ½ lemon*
*1 tbsp freshly shredded basil*
*salt and freshly ground black pepper*
*freshly grated Parmesan cheese, to serve*

## Helpful Hint

Once made and shaped into nests, the pasta can be stored in an airtight container for 1–2 weeks.

# Beetroot Ravioli with Dill Cream Sauce

1 Make the pasta dough according to the recipe on page 16. Wrap in clingfilm and leave to rest for 30 minutes.

2 Heat the olive oil in a large frying pan, add the onion and caraway seeds and cook over a medium heat for 5 minutes, or until the onion is softened and lightly golden. Stir in the beetroot and cook for 5 minutes.

3 Blend the beetroot mixture in a food processor until smooth, then allow to cool. Stir in the ricotta cheese, breadcrumbs, egg yolk and Parmesan cheese. Season the filling to taste with salt and pepper and reserve.

4 Divide the pasta dough into 8 pieces. Roll out as for tagliatelle, but do not cut the sheets in half. Lay 1 sheet on a floured surface and place 5 heaped teaspoons of the filling 2.5 cm/1 inch apart.

5 Dampen around the heaps of filling and lay a second sheet of pasta over the top. Press around the heaps to seal.

6 Cut into squares using a pastry wheel or sharp knife. Put the filled pasta shapes on to a floured tea towel.

7 Bring a large pan of lightly salted water to a rolling boil. Drop the ravioli into the boiling water, return to the boil and cook for 3–4 minutes, until 'al dente'.

8 Meanwhile, heat the walnut oil in a small pan then add the chopped dill and green peppercorns. Remove from the heat, stir in the crème fraîche and season well. Drain the cooked pasta thoroughly and toss with the sauce. Tip into warmed serving dishes and serve immediately.

## INGREDIENTS
### Serves 4–6

fresh pasta (see Fresh Tagliatelle with Courgettes, page 16)
1 tbsp olive oil
1 small onion, peeled and finely chopped
½ tsp caraway seeds
175 g/6 oz cooked beetroot, chopped
175 g/6 oz ricotta cheese
25 g/1 oz fresh white breadcrumbs
1 medium egg yolk
2 tbsp grated Parmesan cheese
salt and freshly ground black pepper
4 tbsp walnut oil
4 tbsp freshly chopped dill
1 tbsp green peppercorns, drained and roughly chopped
6 tbsp crème fraîche

# Gnocchi with Grilled Cherry Tomato Sauce

1 Preheat the grill just before required. Bring a large pan of salted water to the boil, add the potatoes and cook for 20–25 minutes until tender. Drain. Leave until cool enough to handle but still hot, then peel them and place in a large bowl. Mash until smooth then work in the egg, salt and enough of the flour to form a soft dough.

2 With floured hands, roll a spoonful of the dough into a small ball. Flatten the ball slightly on to the back of a large fork, then roll it off the fork to make a little ridged dumpling. Place each gnocchi on to a floured tea towel as you work.

3 Place the tomatoes in a flameproof shallow dish.

Add the garlic, lemon zest, herbs and olive oil. Season to taste with salt and pepper and sprinkle over the sugar. Cook under the pre-heated grill for 10 minutes, or until the tomatoes are charred and tender, stirring once or twice.

4 Meanwhile, bring a large pan of lightly salted water to the boil then reduce to a steady simmer. Dropping in 6–8 gnocchi at a time, cook in batches for 3–4 minutes, or until they begin bobbing up to the surface. Remove with a slotted spoon and drain well on absorbent kitchen paper before transferring to a warmed serving dish; cover with foil. Toss the cooked gnocchi with the tomato sauce. Serve immediately with a little grated Parmesan cheese.

## Helpful Hint

When cooking the gnocchi use a very large pan with at least 1.7 litres/3 pints of water to give them plenty of room so that they do not stick together.

### INGREDIENTS
*Serves 4*

450 g/1 lb floury potatoes, unpeeled
1 medium egg
1 tsp salt
75–90 g/3–3½ oz plain flour
450 g/1 lb mixed red and orange cherry tomatoes, halved lengthways
2 garlic cloves, peeled and finely sliced
zest of ½ lemon, finely grated
1 tbsp freshly chopped thyme
1 tbsp freshly chopped basil
2 tbsp extra virgin olive oil, plus extra for drizzling
salt and freshly ground black pepper
pinch of sugar
freshly grated Parmesan cheese, to serve

# Spinach & Ricotta Gnocchi with Butter & Parmesan

1 Squeeze the excess moisture from the spinach and chop finely. Blend in a food processor with the ricotta cheese, eggs, Parmesan cheese, seasoning and 1 tablespoon of the basil until smooth. Scrape into a bowl then add sufficient flour to form a soft, slightly sticky dough.

2 Bring a large pan of salted water to a rolling boil. Transfer the spinach mixture to a piping bag fitted with a large plain nozzle. As soon as the water is boiling, pipe 10–12 short lengths of the mixture into the water, using a sharp knife to cut the gnocchi as you go.

3 Bring the water back to the boil and cook the gnocchi for 3–4 minutes, or until they begin to rise to the surface. Remove with a slotted spoon, drain on absorbent kitchen paper and transfer to a warmed serving dish. Cook the gnocchi in batches if necessary.

4 Melt the butter in a small frying pan and when foaming add the garlic and remaining basil. Remove from the heat and immediately pour over the cooked gnocchi. Season well with salt and pepper and serve immediately with extra grated Parmesan cheese.

## INGREDIENTS
### Serves 2–4

125 g/4 oz frozen leaf spinach, thawed
225 g/8 oz ricotta cheese
2 small eggs, lightly beaten
50 g/2 oz freshly grated
  Parmesan cheese
salt and freshly ground black
  pepper
2 tbsp freshly chopped basil
50 g/2 oz plain flour
50 g/2 oz unsalted butter
2 garlic cloves, peeled and crushed
Parmesan cheese shavings, to serve

## Food Fact

Ricotta is a crumbly, soft white cheese made from ewes' milk whey, a by-product from the manufacture of Pecorino Romano cheese. The curd is compacted so that the cheese can be cut with a knife. It can be eaten by itself, but normally it is used in dishes such as cheesecake.

# Tagliatelle with Brown Butter, Asparagus & Parmesan

1 If using fresh pasta, prepare the dough according to the recipe on page 16. Cut into tagliatelle, wind into nests and reserve on a floured tea towel until ready to cook.

2 Bring a pan of lightly salted water to the boil. Add the asparagus and cook for 1 minute. Drain immediately, refresh under cold running water and drain again. Pat dry and reserve.

3 Melt the butter in a large frying pan, then add the garlic and hazelnuts and cook over a medium heat until the butter turns golden. Immediately remove from the heat and add the parsley, chives and asparagus. Leave for 2–3 minutes, until the asparagus is heated through.

4 Meanwhile, bring a large pan of lightly salted water to a rolling boil, then add the pasta nests. Cook until 'al dente': 2–3 minutes for fresh pasta and according to the packet instructions for dried pasta. Drain the pasta thoroughly and return to the pan. Add the asparagus mixture and toss together. Season to taste with salt and pepper and tip into a warmed serving dish. Serve immediately with grated Parmesan cheese.

## INGREDIENTS
### Serves 6

fresh pasta (see Fresh Tagliatelle with Courgettes, page 16) or 450 g/1 lb dried tagliatelle, such as the white and green variety
350 g/12 oz asparagus, trimmed and cut into short lengths
75 g/3 oz unsalted butter
1 garlic clove, peeled and sliced
25 g/1 oz flaked hazelnuts or whole hazelnuts, roughly chopped
1 tbsp freshly chopped parsley
1 tbsp freshly snipped chives
salt and freshly ground black pepper
50 g/2 oz freshly grated Parmesan cheese, to serve

## Food Fact

Asparagus is available all year round, but is at its best during May and June. If you buy loose asparagus, rather than pre-packed, choose stems of similar thickness so they will all cook in the same time. It is best to buy them no more than a day before using, but if you need to, you can keep stems fresh by standing them in a little water.

# Pasta with Raw Fennel, Tomato & Red Onions

1 Trim the fennel and slice thinly. Stack the slices and cut into sticks, then cut crosswise again into fine dice. Deseed the tomatoes and chop them finely. Peel and finely chop or crush the garlic. Peel and finely chop or grate the onion.

2 Stack the basil leaves then roll up tightly. Slice crosswise into fine shreds. Finely chop the mint.

3 Place the chopped vegetables and herbs in a medium bowl. Add the olive oil and lemon juice and mix together. Season well with salt and pepper then leave for 30 minutes to allow the flavours to develop.

4 Bring a large pan of salted water to a rolling boil. Add the pasta and cook according to the packet instructions, or until 'al dente'.

5 Drain the cooked pasta thoroughly. Transfer to a warmed serving dish, pour over the vegetable mixture and toss. Serve with the grated Parmesan cheese and extra olive oil to drizzle over.

## INGREDIENTS
*Serves 6*

*1 fennel bulb*
*700 g / 1½ lb tomatoes*
*1 garlic clove*
*¼ small red onion*
*small handful fresh basil*
*small handful fresh mint*
*100 ml / 3½ fl oz extra virgin olive oil, plus extra to serve*
*juice of 1 lemon*
*salt and freshly ground black pepper*
*450 g / 1 lb penne or pennette*
*freshly grated Parmesan cheese, to serve*

## Food Fact

Fennel is a greenish-white bulbous vegetable that has a distinctive aniseed flavour. It is also known as Florence fennel to distinguish it from the herb. When buying fennel, choose a bulb that is well-rounded and as white as possible; the darker green ones may be bitter. Trim off the feathery leaves, chop them finely and use as a garnish.

## Helpful Hint

The vegetables used in this dish are not cooked, but are tossed with the hot pasta. It is important, therefore, that they are chopped finely.

# Spaghetti with Fresh Tomatoes, Chilli & Potatoes

**1** Preheat the grill to high 5 minutes before using. Cook the potatoes in plenty of boiling water until tender but firm. Allow to cool, then peel and cut into cubes.

**2** Blend the garlic, basil and 4 tablespoons of the olive oil in a blender or food processor until the basil is finely chopped, then reserve.

**3** Place the tomatoes, basil and oil mixture in a small bowl, add the chilli and season with salt and pepper to taste. Mix together and reserve the sauce.

**4** Bring a large pan of salted water to a rolling boil, add the spaghetti and cook according to the packet instructions, or until 'al dente'.

**5** Meanwhile, toss the potato cubes with the remaining olive oil and transfer to a baking sheet. Place the potatoes under the preheated grill until they are crisp and golden, turning once or twice, then drain on absorbent kitchen paper.

**6** Drain the pasta thoroughly and transfer to a warmed shallow serving bowl. Add the tomato sauce and the hot potatoes. Toss well and adjust the seasoning to taste. Serve immediately with the grated Parmesan cheese, if using.

## INGREDIENTS
### Serves 6

2 medium potatoes, unpeeled
3 garlic cloves, peeled and crushed
1 small bunch basil, roughly chopped
6 tbsp olive oil
4 large ripe plum tomatoes, skinned, seeded and chopped
1 small red chilli, deseeded and finely chopped
salt and freshly ground black pepper
450 g/1 lb spaghetti
4 tbsp freshly grated Parmesan cheese, to serve (optional)

# Pasta Genovese with Pesto, Green Beans & Potatoes

**1** Put the basil leaves, garlic, pine nuts and Parmesan cheese into a food processor and blend until finely chopped. Transfer the mixture in to a small bowl and stir in the olive oil. Season the pesto to taste with salt and pepper and reserve.

**2** Bring a pan of salted water to boil and cook the potatoes for 12–14 minutes, or until tender. About 4 minutes before the end of the cooking time, add the beans. Drain well and refresh under cold water. Reserve the beans and slice the potatoes thickly, or halve them if small.

**3** Heat the olive oil in a frying pan and add the potatoes. Fry over a medium heat for 5 minutes, or until golden. Add the reserved beans and pesto and cook for a further 2 minutes.

**4** Meanwhile, bring a large pan of lightly salted water to a rolling boil. Cook the pasta shapes according to the packet instructions, or until 'al dente'. Drain thoroughly, return to the pan and add the pesto mixture. Toss well and heat through for 1–2 minutes. Tip into a warmed serving bowl and serve immediately with Parmesan cheese.

## INGREDIENTS
### Serves 6

40 g/1½ oz basil leaves

2 garlic cloves, peeled and crushed

2 tbsp pine nuts, lightly toasted

25 g/1 oz freshly grated
    Parmesan cheese

75 ml/3 fl oz extra virgin
    olive oil

salt and freshly ground pepper

175 g/6 oz new potatoes,
    scrubbed

125 g/4 oz fine French beans,
    trimmed

2 tbsp olive oil

450 g/1 lb pasta shapes

extra freshly grated Parmesan
    cheese, to serve

## Tasty Tip

Classic pesto, as used in this recipe, is always made with fresh basil and pine nuts, but other herb variations work equally well. For a change try a coriander and chilli pesto, replacing the basil with fresh coriander leaves and adding a deseeded and finely chopped red chilli, or try an almond and mint pesto, replacing the pine nuts with blanched almonds and the basil with equal amounts of fresh mint and fresh parsley leaves.

# Tiny Pasta with Fresh Herb Sauce

1 Bring a large pan of lightly salted water to a rolling boil. Add the pasta and cook according to the packet instructions, or until 'al dente'.

2 Meanwhile, place all the herbs, the lemon zest, olive oil, garlic and chilli flakes in a heavy-based pan. Heat gently for 2–3 minutes, or until the herbs turn bright green and become very fragrant. Remove from the heat and season to taste with salt and pepper.

3 Drain the pasta thoroughly, reserving 2–3 tablespoons of the cooking water. Transfer the pasta to a large warmed bowl.

4 Pour the heated herb mixture over the pasta and toss together until thoroughly mixed. Check and adjust the seasoning, adding a little of the pasta cooking water if the pasta mixture seems a bit dry. Transfer to warmed serving dishes and serve immediately with grated Parmesan cheese.

## Helpful Hint

Look out for packets of mixed fresh herbs in the supermarket, if you do not want to buy individual packets or bunches of all the herbs used in this fresh and vibrant sauce. If you cannot find all the herbs listed, you can increase the quantity of some of them as a substitute for others not being used. Do not add more than 1 tablespoon each of thyme or rosemary though, or their flavour may overpower the sauce.

### INGREDIENTS
*Serves 6*

375 g/13 oz tripolini (small bows with rounded ends) or small farfalle
2 tbsp freshly chopped flat-leaf parsley
2 tbsp freshly chopped basil
1 tbsp freshly snipped chives
1 tbsp freshly chopped chervil
1 tbsp freshly chopped tarragon
1 tbsp freshly chopped sage
1 tbsp freshly chopped oregano
1 tbsp freshly chopped marjoram
1 tbsp freshly chopped thyme
1 tbsp freshly chopped rosemary
finely grated zest of 1 lemon
75 ml/3 fl oz extra virgin olive oil
2 garlic cloves, peeled and finely chopped
½ tsp dried chilli flakes
salt and freshly ground black pepper
freshly grated Parmesan cheese, to serve

# Louisiana Prawns & Fettuccine

**1** Heat 2 tablespoons of the olive oil in a large saucepan and add the reserved prawn shells and heads. Fry over a high heat for 2–3 minutes, until the shells turn pink and are lightly browned. Add half the shallots, half the garlic, half the basil and the carrot, onion, celery, parsley and thyme. Season lightly with salt, pepper and cayenne and sauté for 2–3 minutes, stirring often.

**2** Pour in the wine and stir, scraping the pan well. Bring to the boil and simmer for 1 minute, then add the tomatoes. Cook for a further 3–4 minutes then pour in 200 ml/ 7 fl oz water. Bring to the boil, lower the heat and simmer for about 30 minutes, stirring often and using a wooden spoon to mash the prawn shells in order to release as much flavour as possible into the sauce. Lower the heat if the sauce is reducing very quickly.

**3** Strain through a sieve, pressing well to extract as much liquid as possible; there should be about 450 ml/¾ pint. Pour the liquid into a clean pan and bring to the boil, then lower the heat and simmer gently until the liquid is reduced by about half.

**4** Heat the remaining olive oil over a high heat in a clean frying pan and add the peeled prawns. Season lightly and add the lemon juice. Cook for 1 minute, lower the heat and add the remaining shallots and garlic. Cook for 1 minute. Add the sauce and adjust the seasoning.

**5** Meanwhile, bring a large pan of lightly salted water to a rolling boil and add the fettuccine. Cook according to the packet instructions, or until 'al dente', and drain thoroughly. Transfer to a warmed serving dish. Add the sauce and toss well. Garnish with the remaining basil and serve immediately.

## INGREDIENTS
### Serves 4

4 tbsp olive oil

450 g/1 lb raw tiger prawns, washed and peeled, shells and heads reserved

2 shallots, peeled and finely chopped

4 garlic cloves, peeled and finely chopped

large handful fresh basil leaves

1 carrot, peeled and finely chopped

1 onion, peeled and finely chopped

1 celery stick, trimmed and finely chopped

2–3 sprigs fresh parsley

2–3 sprigs fresh thyme

salt and freshly ground black pepper

pinch cayenne pepper

175 ml/6 fl oz dry white wine

450 g/1 lb ripe tomatoes, roughly chopped

juice of ½ lemon, or to taste

350 g/12 oz fettuccine

# Salmon & Roasted Red Pepper Pasta

**1** Preheat the grill to high. Place the salmon in a bowl. Add the shallots, parsley, 3 tablespoons of the olive oil and the lemon juice. Reserve.

**2** Brush the pepper quarters with a little olive oil. Cook them under the preheated grill for 8–10 minutes, or until the skins have blackened and the flesh is tender. Place the peppers in a plastic bag until cool enough to handle. When cooled, peel the peppers and cut into strips. Put the strips into a bowl with the basil and the remaining olive oil and reserve.

**3** Toast the breadcrumbs until dry and lightly browned then toss with the extra virgin olive oil and reserve.

**4** Bring a large pan of salted water to a rolling boil and add the pasta. Cook according to the packet instructions, or until 'al dente'.

**5** Meanwhile, transfer the peppers and their marinade to a hot frying pan. Add the spring onions and cook for 1–2 minutes, or until they have just softened. Add the salmon and its marinade and cook for a further 1–2 minutes, or until the salmon is just cooked. Season to taste with salt and pepper.

**6** Drain the pasta thoroughly and transfer to a warmed serving bowl. Add the salmon mixture and toss gently. Garnish with the breadcrumbs and serve immediately.

## Food Fact

Olive oil is graded according to aroma, flavour, colour and acidity - virgin olive oil has less than 2 per cent acidity, extra virgin olive oil less than 1 per cent.

## INGREDIENTS
### Serves 6

225 g/8 oz skinless and boneless salmon fillet, thinly sliced
3 shallots, peeled and finely chopped
1 tbsp freshly chopped parsley
6 tbsp olive oil
juice of ½ lemon
2 red peppers, deseeded and quartered
handful fresh basil leaves, shredded
50 g/2 oz fresh breadcrumbs
4 tbsp extra virgin olive oil
450 g/1 lb fettuccine or linguine
6 spring onions, trimmed and shredded
salt and freshly ground black pepper

# Spaghettini with Peas, Spring Onions & Mint

1 Soak the saffron in 2 table-spoons hot water while you prepare the sauce. Shell the peas if using fresh ones.

2 Heat 50 g/2 oz of the but-ter in a medium frying pan, add the spring onions and a little salt and cook over a low heat for 2–3 minutes, or until the onions are softened. Add the garlic, then the peas and 100 ml/3 ½ fl oz water. Bring to the boil and cook for 5–6 minutes, or until the peas are just tender. Stir in the mint and keep warm.

3 Blend the remaining butter and the saffron water in a large warmed serving bowl and reserve.

4 Meanwhile, bring a large pan of lightly salted water to a rolling boil and add the spaghettini. Cook according to the packet instructions, or until 'al dente'.

5 Drain thoroughly, reserving 2–3 tablespoons of the pasta cooking water. Tip into a warmed serving bowl, add the pea sauce and toss together gently. Season to taste with salt and pepper. Serve immediately with extra black pepper and grated Parmesan cheese.

## INGREDIENTS
*Serves 6*

*pinch saffron strands*
*700 g/1½ lb fresh peas or 350 g/12 oz frozen petit pois, thawed*
*75 g/3 oz unsalted butter, softened*
*6 spring onions, trimmed and finely sliced*
*salt and freshly ground black pepper*
*1 garlic clove, peeled and finely chopped*
*2 tbsp freshly chopped mint*
*1 tbsp freshly snipped chives*
*450 g/1 lb spaghettini*
*freshly grated Parmesan cheese, to serve*

## Helpful Hint

To develop the full flavour and deep golden colour of the saffron, it should be soaked for at least 20 minutes, so do this well before you start cooking. Saffron is one of the few spices that can be kept for several years, but you must store it in an airtight container, away from light.

# Fusilli with Spicy Tomato & Chorizo Sauce with Roasted Peppers

1 Preheat the grill to high. Brush the pepper quarters with 1 tablespoon of the olive oil, then cook under the pre-heated grill, turning once, for 8–10 minutes, or until the skins have blackened and the flesh is tender. Place the peppers in a plastic bag until cool enough to handle. When cooled, peel the peppers, slice very thinly and reserve.

2 Heat the remaining oil in a frying pan and add the chorizo. Cook over a medium heat for 3–4 minutes, or until starting to brown. Add the garlic and chilli flakes and cook for a further 2–3 minutes.

3 Add the tomatoes, season lightly with salt and pepper then cook gently for about 5 minutes, or until the tomatoes have broken down. Lower the heat and cook for a further 10–15 minutes, or until the sauce has thickened. Add the peppers and heat gently for 1-2 minutes. Adjust the seasoning to taste.

4 Meanwhile, bring a large pan of lightly salted water to a rolling boil. Add the fusilli and cook according to the packet instructions, or until 'al dente'. Drain thoroughly and transfer to a warmed serving dish. Pour over the sauce, sprinkle with basil and serve with Parmesan cheese.

## INGREDIENTS
### Serves 6

4 tbsp olive oil
1 red pepper, deseeded and quartered
1 yellow pepper, deseeded and quartered
175 g/6 oz chorizo (outer skin removed), roughly chopped
2 garlic cloves, peeled and finely chopped
large pinch chilli flakes
700 g/1½ lb ripe tomatoes, skinned and roughly chopped
salt and freshly ground black pepper
450 g/1 lb fusilli
basil leaves, to garnish
freshly grated Parmesan cheese, to serve

## Food Fact

There are two types of chorizo sausage; the dried, salami-type, usually about 5 cm/2 in in diameter, and the slightly softer, semi-dried chorizo, which look like short fat sausages. The latter type is preferable for this recipe. Both types of chorizo are pork sausages containing chilli and paprika, which gives them a vibrant orange-red colour.

# Pasta with Walnut Sauce

1 Place the toasted walnuts in a blender or food processor with the chopped spring onions, one of the garlic cloves and parsley or basil. Blend to a fairly smooth paste, then gradually add 3 tablespoons of the olive oil, until it is well mixed into the paste. Season the walnut paste to taste with salt and pepper and reserve.

2 Bring a large pan of lightly salted water to a rolling boil. Add the broccoli, return to the boil and cook for 2 minutes. Remove the broccoli, using a slotted draining spoon and refresh under cold running water. Drain again and pat dry on absorbent kitchen paper.

3 Bring the water back to a rolling boil. Add the pasta and cook according to the packet instructions, or until 'al dente'.

4 Meanwhile, heat the remaining oil in a frying pan. Add the remaining garlic and chilli. Cook gently for 2 minutes, or until softened. Add the broccoli and walnut paste. Cook for a further 3–4 minutes, or until heated through.

5 Drain the pasta thoroughly and transfer to a large warmed serving bowl. Pour over the walnut and broccoli sauce. Toss together, adjust the seasoning and serve immediately.

## INGREDIENTS
*Serves 4*

50 g/2 oz walnuts, toasted

3 spring onions, trimmed and chopped

2 garlic cloves, peeled and sliced

1 tbsp freshly chopped parsley or basil

5 tbsp extra virgin olive oil

salt and freshly ground black pepper

450 g/1 lb broccoli, cut into florets

350 g/12 oz pasta shapes

1 red chilli, deseeded and finely chopped

## Helpful Hint

There is no hard-and-fast rule about which shape of pasta to use with this recipe; it is really a matter of personal preference. Spirali have been used here, but rigatoni, farfalle, garganelle or pipe rigate would all work well, or you could choose flavoured pasta, such as tomato, or a wholewheat variety for a change.

# Pasta & Bean Soup

1 Heat the olive oil in a heavy-based pan, add the celery and prosciutto and cook gently for 6–8 minutes, or until softened. Add the chopped chilli and potato cubes and cook for a further 10 minutes.

2 Add the garlic to the chilli and potato mixture and cook for 1 minute. Add the chopped tomatoes and simmer for 5 minutes. Stir in two-thirds of the beans, then pour in the chicken or vegetable stock and bring to the boil.

3 Add the pasta shapes to the soup stock and return it to simmering point. Cook the pasta for about 10 minutes, or until 'al dente'.

4 Meanwhile, place the remaining beans in a food processor or blender and blend with enough of the soup stock to make a smooth, thinnish purée.

5 When the pasta is cooked, stir in the puréed beans with the torn basil. Season the soup to taste with salt and pepper. Ladle into serving bowls, garnish with shredded basil and serve immediately with plenty of crusty bread.

## INGREDIENTS
### Serves 4–6

3 tbsp olive oil

2 celery sticks, trimmed and finely chopped

100 g/3½ oz prosciutto or prosciutto di speck, cut in pieces

1 red chilli, deseeded and finely chopped

2 large potatoes, peeled and cut into 2.5 cm/1 in cubes

2 garlic cloves, peeled and finely chopped

3 ripe plum tomatoes, skinned and chopped

1 x 400 g cans borlotti beans, drained and rinsed

1 litre/1¼ pints chicken or vegetable stock

100 g/3½ oz pasta shapes

large handful basil leaves, torn

salt and freshly ground black pepper

shredded basil leaves, to garnish

crusty bread, to serve

## Food Fact

Oval borlotti beans have red-streaked, pinkish-brown skin. They have a moist texture and a bitter-sweet flavour, which makes them excellent in soups. Other canned beans may be used if preferred. Try pinto beans, a smaller, paler version of the borlotti bean, or cannellini beans, which have a soft creamy texture.

# Gnocchetti with Broccoli & Bacon Sauce

*nutmeg good.*

1 Bring a large pan of salted water to the boil. Add the broccoli florets and cook for about 8–10 minutes, or until very soft. Drain thoroughly, allow to cool slightly then chop finely and reserve.

2 Heat the olive oil in a heavy-based pan, add the pancetta or bacon and cook over a medium heat for 5 minutes, or until golden and crisp. Add the onion and cook for a further 5 minutes, or until soft and lightly golden. Add the garlic and cook for 1 minute.

3 Transfer the chopped broccoli to the bacon or pancetta mixture and pour in the milk. Bring slowly to the boil and simmer rapidly for about 15 minutes, or until reduced to a creamy texture.

4 Meanwhile, bring a large pan of lightly salted water to a rolling boil. Add the pasta and cook according to the packet instructions, or until 'al dente'.

5 Drain the pasta thoroughly, reserving a little of the cooking water. Add the pasta and the Parmesan cheese to the broccoli mixture. Toss, adding enough of the reserved cooking water to make a creamy sauce. Season to taste with salt and pepper. Serve immediately with extra Parmesan cheese.

### INGREDIENTS
*Serves 6*

*450 g/1 lb broccoli florets*
*4 tbsp olive oil*
*50 g/2 oz pancetta or smoked bacon, finely chopped*
*1 small onion, peeled and finely chopped*
*3 garlic cloves, peeled and sliced*
*200 ml/7 fl oz milk*
*450 g/1 lb gnocchetti (little elongated ribbed shells)*
*50 g/2 oz freshly grated Parmesan cheese, plus extra to serve*
*salt and freshly ground black pepper*

## Food Fact

Pancetta is an Italian streaky bacon that may be either smoked or unsmoked. You can buy it sliced or in a piece, but it is often sold pre-packed, cut into tiny cubes ready for cooking. Thickly cut, rindless smoked streaky bacon makes a good alternative.

# Penne with Artichokes, Bacon & Mushrooms

**1** Heat the olive oil in a frying pan and add the pancetta or bacon and the onion. Cook over a medium heat for 8–10 minutes, or until the bacon is crisp and the onion is just golden. Add the mushrooms and garlic and cook for a further 5 minutes, or until softened.

**2** Add the artichoke hearts to the mushroom mixture and cook for 3–4 minutes. Pour in the wine, bring to the boil then simmer rapidly until the liquid is reduced and syrupy.

**3** Pour in the chicken stock, bring to the boil then simmer rapidly for about 5 minutes, or until slightly reduced. Reduce the heat slightly, then slowly stir in the double cream and Parmesan cheese. Season the sauce to taste with salt and pepper.

**4** Meanwhile, bring a large pan of lightly salted water to a rolling boil. Add the pasta and cook according to the packet instructions, or until 'al dente'.

**5** Drain the pasta thoroughly and transfer to a large warmed serving dish. Pour over the sauce and toss together. Garnish with shredded basil and serve with extra Parmesan cheese.

## INGREDIENTS
*Serves 6*

2 tbsp olive oil

75 g/3 oz smoked bacon or pancetta, chopped

1 small onion, peeled and finely sliced

125 g/4 oz chestnut mushrooms, wiped and sliced

2 garlic cloves, peeled and finely chopped

400 g/14 oz can artichoke hearts, drained and halved or quartered if large

100 ml/3½ fl oz dry white wine

100 ml/3½ fl oz chicken stock

3 tbsp double cream

50 g/2 oz freshly grated Parmesan cheese, plus extra to serve

salt and freshly ground black pepper

450 g/1 lb penne

shredded basil leaves, to garnish

## Tasty Tip

Brown-capped chestnut mushrooms are similar in appearance to cultivated button mushrooms, but they have a rich orange-brown colour and a slightly stronger, nutty flavour. Tiny, baby chestnut mushrooms are sometimes available and could be used whole or halved in this recipe.

# Fettuccine with Wild Mushrooms & Prosciutto

1 Place the dried mushrooms in a small bowl and pour over the hot chicken stock. Leave to soak for 15–20 minutes, or until the mushrooms have softened.

2 Meanwhile, heat the olive oil in a large frying pan. Add the onion and cook for 5 minutes over a medium heat, or until softened. Add the garlic and cook for 1 minute, then add the prosciutto and cook for a further minute.

3 Drain the dried mushrooms, reserving the soaking liquid. Roughly chop and add to the frying pan together with the fresh mushrooms. Cook over a high heat for 5 minutes, stirring often, or until softened. Strain the mushroom soaking liquid into the pan.

4 Meanwhile, bring a large pan of lightly salted water to a rolling boil. Add the pasta and cook according to the packet instructions, or until 'al dente'.

5 Stir the crème fraîche and chopped parsley into the mushroom mixture and heat through gently. Season to taste with salt and pepper. Drain the pasta well, transfer to a large warmed serving dish and pour over the sauce. Serve immediately with grated Parmesan cheese.

## INGREDIENTS
### Serves 6

15 g/½ oz dried porcini mushrooms

150 ml/¼ pint hot chicken stock

2 tbsp olive oil

1 small onion, peeled and finely chopped

2 garlic cloves, peeled and finely chopped

4 slices prosciutto, chopped or torn

225 g/8 oz mixed wild or cultivated mushrooms, wiped and sliced if necessary

450 g/1 lb fettuccine

3 tbsp crème fraîche

2 tbsp freshly chopped parsley

salt and freshly ground black pepper

freshly grated Parmesan cheese, to serve (optional)

## Food Fact

Prosciutto is produced from pigs fed on whey, a by-product of the local Parmesan cheese industry. The ham is dry cured, then weighted to flatten it and give it a dense texture. The delicious flavour develops during the year it is allowed to mature. It is always served in paper-thin slices, either raw or lightly fried.

# Tagliarini with Broad Beans, Saffron & Crème Fraîche

1 If using fresh broad beans, bring a pan of lightly salted water to the boil. Pod the beans and drop them into the boiling water for 1 minute. Drain and refresh under cold water. Drain again. Remove the outer skin of the beans and discard. If using thawed frozen broad beans, remove and discard the skins. Reserve the peeled beans.

2 Heat the olive oil in a saucepan. Add the peeled broad beans and the garlic and cook gently for 2–3 minutes. Stir in the basil, the crème fraîche and the pinch of saffron strands and simmer for 1 minute.

3 Meanwhile, bring a large pan of lightly salted water to a rolling boil. Add the pasta and cook according to the packet instructions, or until 'al dente'. Drain the pasta well and add to the sauce. Toss together and season to taste with salt and pepper.

4 Transfer the pasta and sauce to a warmed serving dish. Sprinkle with snipped chives and serve immediately with Parmesan cheese.

## INGREDIENTS
*Serves 2–3*

225 g/8 oz fresh young broad
  beans in pods or 100 g/3½ oz
  frozen broad beans, thawed
1 tbsp olive oil
1 garlic clove, peeled and chopped
small handful basil leaves,
  shredded
200 ml/7 fl oz crème fraîche
large pinch saffron strands
350 g/12 oz tagliarini
salt and freshly ground black
  pepper
1 tbsp freshly snipped chives
freshly grated Parmesan cheese, to
  serve

## Helpful Hint

If you buy fresh broad beans in their pods (they are available from May to July), look for smooth, plump, bright green pods and use within two days of purchase; they should be cooked the same day as shelling. The skins on the beans become tougher as they age, so if the beans are very young and fresh, there is no need to peel them.

# Linguine with Fennel, Crab & Chervil

**1** Bring a large pan of lightly salted water to a rolling boil. Add the pasta and cook according to the packet instructions, or until 'al dente'.

**2** Meanwhile, heat the butter in a large saucepan. Add the carrots, shallots, celery, fennel and three-quarters of the chopped spring onions. Cook the vegetables gently for 8–10 minutes, or until tender, stirring frequently and ensuring that they do not brown.

**3** Add the double cream and chopped chervil to the vegetable mixture. Scrape the crab meat over the sauce, then stir to mix the sauce ingredients.

**4** Season the sauce to taste with salt and pepper and stir in the lemon juice. Drain the pasta thoroughly and transfer to a large warmed serving dish. Pour over the sauce and toss. Garnish with extra chervil, the remaining spring onions and a sprig of dill. Serve immediately.

## Helpful Hint

If you prefer to prepare a cooked crab yourself, start by twisting off the legs and claws, then cracking them open and removing the meat. Next, turn the crab on to its back and twist off the bony, pointed flap. Put the tip of a knife between the main shell and where the legs and claws were attached, twist the blade to lift up and remove, then scrape out the brown meat in the main shell. Pull away and discard the grey, soft gills. Split the body in half and, using a skewer, remove all the white meat from the cavities. An average-sized crab should produce about 225 g/8 oz of white and brown meat.

### INGREDIENTS
*Serves 6*

*450g/1 lb linguine*
*25 g/1 oz butter*
*2 carrots, peeled and finely diced*
*2 shallots, peeled and finely diced*
*2 celery sticks, trimmed and finely diced*
*1 bulb fennel, trimmed and finely diced*
*6 spring onions, trimmed and finely chopped*
*300 ml/½ pint double cream*
*3 tbsp freshly chopped chervil*
*1 large cooked crab plus extra for garnish*
*salt and freshly ground pepper*
*juice of ½ lemon, or to taste*
*sprig of dill, to garnish*

# Farfalle with Smoked Trout in a Dill & Vodka Sauce

1 Bring a large pan of lightly salted water to a rolling boil. Add the pasta and cook according to the packet instructions, or until 'al dente'.

2 Meanwhile, cut the smoked trout into thin slivers, using scissors. Sprinkle lightly with the lemon juice and reserve.

3 Place the cream, mustard, chopped dill and vodka in a small pan. Season lightly with salt and pepper. Bring the contents of the pan to the boil and simmer gently for 2-3 minutes, or until slightly thickened.

4 Drain the cooked pasta thoroughly, then return to the pan. Add the smoked trout to the dill and vodka sauce, then pour over the pasta. Toss gently until the pasta is coated and the trout evenly mixed.

5 Spoon into a warmed serving dish or on to individual plates. Garnish with sprigs of dill and serve immediately.

## INGREDIENTS
*Serves 4*

*400 g/14 oz farfalle*
*150 g/5 oz smoked trout*
*2 tsp lemon juice*
*200 ml/7 fl oz double cream*
*2 tsp wholegrain mustard*
*2 tbsp freshly chopped dill*
*4 tbsp vodka*
*salt and freshly ground black pepper*
*sprigs of dill, to garnish*

## Food Fact

Two types of smoked trout are available. One resembles smoked salmon in colour, texture and flavour, and can be cut into thin slivers as shown here. Equally delicious is hot smoked rainbow trout, which is available as a whole fish or in fillets. These should be skinned and the bones should be removed before use. The flesh can then be broken into large flakes. Smoked trout is fairly salty, so the sauce requires a minimal amount of seasoning with salt.

# Pappardelle with Smoked Haddock & Blue Cheese Sauce

1 Place the smoked haddock in a saucepan with 1 bay leaf and pour in the milk. Bring to the boil slowly, cover and simmer for 6–7 minutes, or until the fish is opaque. Remove and roughly flake the fish, discarding the skin and any bones. Strain the milk and reserve.

2 Bring a large pan of lightly salted water to a rolling boil. Add the pasta and cook according to the packet instructions, or until 'al dente'.

3 Meanwhile, place the butter, flour and single cream or milk if preferred, in a pan and stir to mix. Stir in the reserved warm milk and add the remain-

ing bay leaf. Bring to the boil, whisking all the time until smooth and thick. Gently simmer for 3–4 minutes, stirring frequently. Discard the bay leaf.

4 Add the Dolcelatte or Gorgonzola cheese to the sauce. Heat gently, stirring until melted. Add the flaked haddock and season to taste with nutmeg and salt and pepper.

5 Drain the pasta thoroughly and return to the pan. Add the sauce and toss gently to coat, taking care not to break up the flakes of fish. Tip into a warmed serving bowl, sprinkle with toasted walnuts and parsley and serve immediately.

## Tasty Tip

Dolcelatte is an Italian, semi-soft, blue-veined cheese made from cows' milk. It has a smooth creamy texture and a delicate taste. For a more strongly flavoured blue cheese sauce, a young Gorgonzola, Roquefort or blue Stilton can be used instead.

### INGREDIENTS
*Serves 4*

350 g/12 oz smoked haddock
2 bay leaves
300 ml/½ pint milk
400 g/14 oz pappardelle or tagliatelle
25 g/1 oz butter
25 g/1 oz plain flour
150 ml/¼ pint single cream or extra milk
125 g/4 oz Dolcelatte cheese or Gorgonzola, cut into small pieces
¼ tsp freshly grated nutmeg
salt and freshly ground black pepper
40 g/1½ oz toasted walnuts, chopped
1 tbsp freshly chopped parsley

# Special Seafood Lasagne

1 Preheat the oven to 200°C/ 400°F/Gas Mark 6, 15 minutes before cooking. Place the haddock in a pan with the wine, fish stock, onion and bay leaf. Bring to the boil slowly, cover and simmer gently for 5 minutes, or until the fish is opaque. Remove and flake the fish, discarding any bones. Strain the cooking juices and reserve.

2 Melt 50 g/2 oz of the butter in a large saucepan. Add the leeks and garlic and cook gently for 10 minutes. Remove from the pan, using a slotted draining spoon, and reserve.

3 Melt the remaining butter in a small saucepan. Stir in the flour, then gradually whisk in the cream, off the heat, followed by the reserved cooking juices. Bring to the boil slowly, whisking until thickened. Stir in the dill and season to taste with salt and pepper.

4 Spoon a little of the sauce into the base of a buttered 2.8 litre/5 pint shallow oven-proof dish. Top with a layer of lasagne, followed by the haddock, seafood cocktail and leeks. Spoon over enough sauce to cover. Continue layering up, finishing with sheets of lasagne topped with sauce.

5 Sprinkle over the grated Gruyère cheese and bake in the preheated oven for 40–45 minutes, or until golden-brown and bubbling. Serve immediately.

## INGREDIENTS
*Serves 4–6*

*450 g/1 lb fresh haddock fillet, skinned*
*150 ml/¼ pint dry white wine*
*150 ml/¼ pint fish stock*
*½ onion, peeled and thickly sliced*
*1 bay leaf*
*75 g/3 oz butter*
*350 g/12 oz leeks, trimmed and thickly sliced*
*1 garlic clove, peeled and crushed*
*25 g/1 oz plain flour*
*150 ml/¼ pint single cream*
*2 tbsp freshly chopped dill*
*salt and freshly ground black pepper*
*8–12 sheets dried lasagne verde, cooked*
*225 g/8 oz ready-cooked seafood cocktail*
*50 g/2 oz Gruyère cheese, grated*

## Helpful Hint

Cook the lasagne in a large pan of boiling salted water with 1 teaspoon olive oil for about 7 minutes, or according to the packet instructions. Do this even if using pasta labelled pre-cooked. Drain thoroughly and rinse briefly under cold water.

# Tuna & Macaroni Timbales

1 Preheat the oven to 180° C/ 350°F/Gas Mark 4, 10 minutes before cooking. Oil and line the bases of 4 individual 150 ml/ ¼ pint timbales or ovenproof cups with non-stick baking parchment and stand in a small roasting tin.

2 Bring a large pan of lightly salted water to a rolling boil. Add the macaroni and cook according to the packet instructions, or until 'al dente'. Drain the cooked pasta thoroughly.

3 Flake the tuna fish and mix with the macaroni. Divide between the timbales or cups.

4 Pour the single and double cream into a small saucepan. Bring to the boil slowly, remove from the heat and stir in the Gruyère cheese until melted. Allow to cool for 1–2 minutes, then whisk into the beaten egg and season lightly with salt and

pepper. Pour the mixture over the tuna fish and macaroni and cover each timbale with a small piece of tinfoil.

5 Pour enough hot water into the roasting tin to come halfway up the timbales. Place in the preheated oven and cook for 25 minutes. Remove the timbales from the water and allow to stand for 5 minutes.

6 For the tomato dressing, whisk together the mustard and vinegar in a small bowl, using a fork. Gradually whisk in the sunflower and nut oils, then stir in the chopped tomatoes and the snipped chives.

7 Unmould the timbales on to warmed serving plates and spoon the tomato dressing over the top and around the bottom. Garnish with fresh chives and serve immediately.

## INGREDIENTS
*Serves 4*

*125 g/4 oz macaroni*
*200 g can tuna in brine, drained*
*150 ml/¼ pint single cream*
*150 ml/¼ pint double cream*
*50 g/2 oz Gruyère cheese, grated*
*3 medium eggs, lightly beaten*
*salt and freshly ground black*
   *pepper*
*fresh chives, to garnish*

## FRESH TOMATO DRESSING:

*1 tsp Dijon mustard*
*1 tsp red wine vinegar*
*2 tbsp sunflower oil*
*1 tbsp hazelnut or walnut oil*
*350 g/12 oz firm ripe tomatoes,*
   *skinned, deseeded and chopped*
*2 tbsp freshly snipped chives*

## Tasty Tip

Other fish can be used to make these pasta timbales. Try a 200 g can of white crab meat, rinsed and drained, or pink salmon with all the bones removed.

# Saucy Cod & Pasta Bake

1 Preheat the oven to 200°C/ 400°F/Gas Mark 6, 15 minutes before cooking. Cut the cod into bite-sized pieces and reserve.

2 Heat the sunflower oil in a large saucepan, add the onion and bacon and cook for 7–8 minutes. Add the mushrooms and celery and cook for 5 minutes, or until fairly soft.

3 Add the courgettes and tomatoes to the bacon mixture and pour in the fish stock or wine. Bring to the boil, then simmer uncovered for 5 minutes, or until the sauce has thickened slightly. Remove from the heat and stir in the cod pieces and the tarragon. Season to taste

with salt and pepper, then spoon into a large oiled baking dish.

4 Meanwhile, bring a large pan of lightly salted water to a rolling boil. Add the pasta shells and cook, according to the packet instructions, or until 'al dente'.

5 For the topping, place the butter and flour in a saucepan and pour in the milk. Bring to the boil slowly, whisking until thickened and smooth.

6 Drain the pasta thoroughly, and stir into the sauce. Spoon carefully over the fish and vegetables. Place in the preheated oven and bake for 20–25 minutes, or until the top is lightly browned and bubbling.

## Helpful Hint

If you are short of time, you can make a simpler topping. Beat together 2 eggs, 3 tablespoons Greek-style yogurt and 3 tablespoons double cream; season to taste with salt and pepper. Add the drained pasta and mix well. Spoon on top of the fish and vegetables and bake as above for 15–20 minutes, or until the top is set and golden brown.

*INGREDIENTS*
*Serves 4*

*450 g/1 lb cod fillets, skinned*
*2 tbsp sunflower oil*
*1 onion, peeled and chopped*
*4 rashers smoked streaky bacon, rind removed and chopped*
*150 g/5 oz baby button mushrooms, wiped*
*2 celery sticks, trimmed and thinly sliced*
*2 small courgettes, halved lengthwise and sliced*
*400 g can chopped tomatoes*
*100 ml/3½ fl oz fish stock or dry white wine*
*1 tbsp freshly chopped tarragon*
*salt and freshly ground black pepper*

*PASTA TOPPING:*
*225–275 g/8–10 oz pasta shells*
*25 g/1 oz butter*
*4 tbsp plain flour*
*450 ml/¾ pint milk*

# Pasta Provençale

1 Heat the olive oil in a large saucepan, add the garlic and onion and cook gently for 5 minutes. Add the fennel and cook for a further 5 minutes. Stir in the chopped tomatoes and rosemary sprig. Half-cover the pan and simmer for 10 minutes.

2 Cut the monkfish into bite-sized pieces and sprinkle with the lemon juice. Add to the tomatoes, cover and simmer gently for 5 minutes, or until the fish is opaque.

3 Meanwhile, bring a large pan of lightly salted water to a rolling boil. Add the pasta and cook according to the packet instructions, or until 'al dente'. Drain the pasta thoroughly and return to the saucepan.

4 Remove the rosemary from the tomato sauce. Stir in the black olives, flageolet beans and chopped oregano, then season to taste with salt and pepper. Add the sauce to the pasta and toss gently together to coat, taking care not to break up the monkfish. Tip into a warmed serving bowl. Garnish with rosemary and oregano sprigs and serve immediately.

## INGREDIENTS
### Serves 4

2 tbsp olive oil
1 garlic clove, peeled and crushed
1 onion, peeled and finely chopped
1 small fennel bulb, trimmed and halved and thinly sliced
400 g can chopped tomatoes
1 rosemary sprig, plus extra sprig to garnish
350 g/12 oz monkfish, skinned
2 tsp lemon juice
400 g/14 oz gnocchi pasta
50 g/2 oz pitted black olives
200 g can flageolet beans, drained and rinsed
1 tbsp freshly chopped oregano, plus sprig to garnish
salt and freshly ground black pepper

## Helpful Hint

Only the tail of the monkfish is eaten and this is usually sold skinned. It has a firm, very white, almost meaty flesh and just one bone running down the middle. It may still have a tough transparent membrane covering it, which should be carefully removed before cooking. A less expensive firm white fish, such as haddock, may be used if preferred.

# Seared Salmon
# & Lemon Linguine

**1** Brush the salmon fillets with the sunflower oil, sprinkle with crushed peppercorns and press on firmly and reserve.

**2** Bring a large pan of lightly salted water to a rolling boil. Add the linguine and cook according to the packet instructions, or until 'al dente'.

**3** Meanwhile, melt the butter in a saucepan and cook the shredded spring onions gently for 2–3 minutes, or until soft. Stir in the soured cream and the lemon zest and remove from the heat.

**4** Preheat a griddle or heavy-based frying pan until very hot. Add the salmon and sear for 1½–2 minutes on each side. Remove from the pan and allow to cool slightly.

**5** Bring the soured cream sauce to the boil and stir in the Parmesan cheese and lemon juice. Drain the pasta thoroughly and return to the pan. Pour over the sauce and toss gently to coat.

**6** Spoon the pasta on to warmed serving plates and top with the salmon fillets. Serve immediately with sprigs of dill and lemon slices.

## Helpful Hint

If you are unable to find soured cream, stir 1 teaspoon lemon juice into 300 ml/½ pint of double cream and leave at room temperature for 20 minutes before using. For a less rich and lower fat version of the sauce, use Greek-style yogurt instead, but do not boil as in step 5. Instead, heat gently with the Parmesan cheese until the cheese melts, then pour over the pasta and toss to coat in the sauce, as above.

### INGREDIENTS
*Serves 4*

*4 small skinless salmon fillets, each about 75 g/3 oz*
*2 tsp sunflower oil*
*½ tsp mixed or black peppercorns, crushed*
*400 g/14 oz linguine*
*15 g/½ oz unsalted butter*
*1 bunch spring onions, trimmed and shredded*
*300 ml/½ pint soured cream*
*zest of 1 lemon, finely grated*
*50 g/2 oz freshly grated Parmesan cheese*
*1 tbsp lemon juice*
*pinch of salt*

### TO GARNISH:
*dill sprigs*
*lemon slices*

# Tagliatelle with Tuna & Anchovy Tapenade

1 Bring a large pan of lightly salted water to a rolling boil. Add the tagliatelle and cook according to the packet instructions, or until 'al dente'.

2 Meanwhile, place the tuna fish, anchovy fillets, olives and capers in a food processor with the lemon juice and 2 tablespoons of the olive oil and blend for a few seconds until roughly chopped.

3 With the motor running, pour in the remaining olive oil in a steady stream; the resulting mixture should be slightly chunky rather than smooth.

4 Spoon the sauce into a bowl, stir in the chopped parsley and season to taste with black pepper. Check the taste of the sauce and add a little more lemon juice, if required.

5 Drain the pasta thoroughly. Pour the sauce into the pan and cook over a low heat for 1–2 minutes to warm through.

6 Return the drained pasta to the pan and mix together with the sauce. Tip into a warmed serving bowl or spoon on to warm individual plates. Garnish with sprigs of flat-leaf parsley and serve immediately.

## INGREDIENTS
*Serves 4*

*400 g / 14 oz tagliatelle*
*125 g can tuna fish in oil, drained*
*45 g / 1¾ oz can anchovy fillets, drained*
*150 g / 5 oz pitted black olives*
*2 tbsp capers in brine, drained*
*2 tsp lemon juice*
*100 ml / 3½ fl oz olive oil*
*2 tbsp freshly chopped parsley*
*freshly ground black pepper*
*sprigs of flat-leaf parsley, to garnish*

## Food Fact

Capers are the flower buds of the caper bush, which grows throughout the Mediterranean region. The buds are picked before they open and preserved in vinegar and salt. The word tapenade (a mixture of capers, olives and fish, usually anchovies, pounded to a paste with olive oil) comes from the Provençal word for capers – *tapeno*.

# Hot Prawn Noodles with Sesame Dressing

1 Pour the vegetable stock into a large saucepan and bring to the boil. Add the egg noodles, stir once, then cook according to the packet instructions, usually about 3 minutes.

2 Meanwhile, heat the sunflower oil in a small frying pan. Add the chopped garlic and chilli and cook gently for a few seconds. Add the sesame seeds and cook, stirring continuously, for 1 minute, or until golden.

3 Add the soy sauce, sesame oil and prawns to the frying pan. Continue cooking for a few seconds, until the mixture is just starting to bubble, then remove immediately from the heat.

4 Drain the noodles thoroughly and return to the pan. Add the prawns in the dressing mixture, and the chopped coriander and season to taste with black pepper. Toss gently to coat the noodles with the hot dressing.

5 Tip into a warmed serving bowl or spoon on to individual plates and serve immediately, garnished with sprigs of fresh coriander.

## Food Fact

There are two types of sesame oil that feature frequently in Oriental cooking – the pale and light version, made from untoasted seeds, and the rich dark kind, made from toasted seeds. The latter has a very strong nutty flavour, which can be overpowering in large quantities. If you use the toasted variety in the dressing for this dish, use just 1 tablespoon mixed together with 1 tablespoon of groundnut or sunflower oil.

## INGREDIENTS
### Serves 4

600 ml/1 pint vegetable stock
350 g/12 oz Chinese egg noodles
1 tbsp sunflower oil
1 garlic clove, peeled and very finely chopped
1 red chilli, deseeded and finely chopped
3 tbsp sesame seeds
3 tbsp dark soy sauce
2 tbsp sesame oil
175 g/6 oz shelled cooked prawns
3 tbsp freshly chopped coriander
freshly ground black pepper
fresh coriander sprigs, to garnish

# Pan-fried Scallops & Pasta

**1** Rinse the scallops and pat dry on absorbent kitchen paper. Place in a bowl and add the olive oil, crushed garlic and thyme. Cover and chill in the refrigerator until ready to cook.

**2** Bring a large pan of lightly salted water to a rolling boil. Add the penne and cook according to the packet instructions, or until 'al dente'.

**3** Meanwhile, make the dressing. Place the sun-dried tomatoes into a small bowl or glass jar and add the vinegars, tomato paste, sugar, salt and pepper. Whisk well, then pour into a food processor.

**4** With the motor running, pour in the sun-dried tomato oil and olive oil in a steady stream to make a thick, smooth dressing.

**5** Preheat a large, dry cast-iron griddle pan over a high heat for about 5 minutes. Lower the heat to medium then add the scallops to the pan. Cook for 1½ minutes on each side. Remove from the pan.

**6** Drain the pasta thoroughly and return to the pan. Add the sliced sun-dried tomatoes and dressing and toss. Divide between individual serving plates, top each portion with 4 scallops, garnish with fresh thyme or oregano sprigs and serve immediately.

## Handy Hint

Try to buy ready-shelled fresh scallops. If you buy in shells, follow this quick and simple method of opening them. Preheat the oven to 150°C/300°F/Gas Mark 2. Place the scallops on a baking sheet, rounded-sided down and put this in the oven for about 10 minutes, or until the shells just open. When pan-frying the scallops, take care not to overcook them, or they will lose their moist, tender texture.

### INGREDIENTS
*Serves 4*

*16 large scallops, shelled*
*1 tbsp olive oil*
*1 garlic clove, peeled and crushed*
*1 tsp freshly chopped thyme*
*400 g/14 oz penne*
*4 sun-dried tomatoes in oil, drained and thinly sliced*
*thyme or oregano sprigs, to garnish*

### TOMATO DRESSING:

*2 sun-dried tomatoes in oil, drained and chopped*
*1 tbsp red wine vinegar*
*2 tsp balsamic vinegar*
*1 tsp sun-dried tomato paste*
*1 tsp caster sugar*
*salt and freshly ground black pepper*
*2 tbsp oil from a jar of sun-dried tomatoes*
*2 tbsp olive oil*

# Smoked Mackerel & Pasta Frittata

**1** Preheat the grill to high just before cooking. Bring a pan of lightly salted water to a rolling boil. Add the pasta and cook according to the packet instructions, or until 'al dente'. Drain thoroughly and reserve.

**2** Remove the skin from the mackerel and break the fish into large flakes, discarding any bones, and reserve.

**3** Place the eggs, milk, mustard and parsley in a bowl and whisk together. Season with just a little salt and plenty of freshly ground black pepper and reserve.

**4** Melt the butter in a large, heavy-based frying pan.

Cook the spring onions gently for 3–4 minutes, until soft. Pour in the egg mixture, then add the drained pasta, peas and half of the mackerel.

**5** Gently stir the mixture in the pan for 1–2 minutes, or until beginning to set. Stop stirring and cook for about 1 minute until the underneath is golden-brown.

**6** Scatter the remaining mackerel over the frittata, followed by the grated cheese. Place under the preheated grill for about 1½ minutes, or until golden-brown and set. Cut into wedges and serve immediately with salad and crusty bread.

## INGREDIENTS
*Serves 4*

25 g/1 oz tricolore pasta spirals
   or shells
225 g/8 oz smoked mackerel
6 medium eggs
3 tbsp milk
2 tsp wholegrain mustard
2 tbsp freshly chopped parsley
salt and freshly ground black
   pepper
25 g/1 oz unsalted butter
6 spring onions, trimmed and
   diagonally sliced
50 g/2 oz frozen peas, thawed
75 g/3 oz mature Cheddar
   cheese, grated

### TO SERVE:
green salad
warm crusty bread

## Food Fact

A frittata is a thick-set Italian omelette, similar
to the Spanish tortilla, which may be served hot or
cold cut into wedges or fingers. To ensure even cooking,
it should be cooked very slowly over a low heat and
gently stirred only until the mixture starts to set.

# Crispy Cod Cannelloni

1 Add 1 teaspoon of the olive oil to a large pan of lightly salted water and bring to a rolling boil. Add the cannelloni tubes and cook, uncovered, for 5 minutes. Drain and leave in a bowl of cold water.

2 Melt the butter with the remaining oil in a saucepan. Add the mushrooms and leeks and cook gently for 5 minutes. Turn up the heat and cook for 1–2 minutes, or until the mixture is fairly dry. Add the cod and cook, stirring, for 2–3 minutes, or until the fish is opaque.

3 Add the cream cheese to the pan and stir until melted. Season to taste with salt and pepper, then leave the cod mixture to cool.

4 Drain the cannelloni. Using a piping bag without a nozzle or a spoon, fill the cannelloni with the cod mixture.

5 Mix the Parmesan cheese and breadcrumbs together on a plate. Dip the filled cannelloni into the flour, then into the beaten egg and finally into the breadcrumb mixture. Dip the ends twice to ensure they are thoroughly coated. Chill in the refrigerator for 30 minutes.

6 Heat the oil for deep frying to 180°C/350°F. Fry the stuffed cannelloni in batches for 2–3 minutes, or until the coating is crisp and golden-brown. Drain on absorbent kitchen paper and serve immediately with fresh herbs or salad leaves.

## INGREDIENTS
### Serves 4

1 tbsp olive oil
8 dried cannelloni tubes
25 g/1 oz unsalted butter
225 g/8 oz button mushrooms, thinly sliced
175 g/6 oz leeks, trimmed and finely chopped
175 g/6 oz cod, skinned and diced
175 g/6 oz cream cheese
salt and freshly ground black pepper
15 g/½ oz Parmesan cheese, grated
50 g/2 oz fine fresh white breadcrumbs
3 tbsp plain flour
1 medium egg, lightly beaten
oil for deep frying
fresh herbs or salad leaves, to serve

## Handy Hint

Use a deep, heavy-based pan or a deep-fat fryer for deep-frying. Fill the pan to no more than one-third full with oil. If you do not have a food thermometer to check the oil's temperature, test by dropping in a cube of stale bread; it will turn golden-brown in 40 seconds, when the oil is hot enough.

# Spaghetti alle Vongole

1 Soak the clams in lightly salted cold water for 8 hours before required, changing the water once or twice. Scrub the clams, removing any that have broken shells or that remain open when tapped.

2 Place the prepared clams in a large saucepan and pour in the wine. Cover with a tight-fitting lid and cook over a medium heat for 5–6 minutes, shaking the pan occasionally, until the shells have opened.

3 Strain the clams and cooking juices through a sieve lined with muslin and reserve. Discard any clams that have remained unopened.

4 Heat the olive oil in a saucepan and fry the onion and garlic gently for 10 minutes, or until very soft.

5 Meanwhile, bring a large pan of lightly salted water to a rolling boil. Add the spaghetti and cook according to the packet instructions, or until 'al dente'.

6 Add the cooked clams to the onions and garlic and pour in the reserved cooking juices. Bring to the boil, then add the parsley and basil and season to taste with salt and black pepper.

7 Drain the spaghetti thoroughly. Return to the pan and add the clams with their sauce. Toss together gently, then tip into a large warmed serving bowl or into individual bowls. Serve immediately, sprinkled with oregano leaves.

## INGREDIENTS
*Serves 4*

1.8 kg / 4 lb small fresh clams
6 tbsp dry white wine
2 tbsp olive oil
1 small onion, peeled and finely
  chopped
2 garlic cloves, peeled and crushed
400 g / 14 oz spaghetti
2 tbsp freshly chopped parsley
2 tbsp freshly chopped or torn
  basil
salt and freshly ground black
  pepper
oregano leaves, to garnish

## Handy Hint

Cook and eat clams within 24 hours of buying them. Steam them until the shells have just opened, as overcooking will toughen them.

# Seafood Parcels with Pappardelle & Coriander Pesto

1 Preheat the oven to 180°C/ 350° F/Gas Mark 4, 10 minutes before cooking. To make the pesto, blend the coriander leaves, garlic, pine nuts and lemon juice with 1 tablespoon of the olive oil to a smooth paste in a food processor. With the motor running slowly add the remaining oil. Stir the Parmesan cheese into the pesto and season to taste with salt and pepper.

2 Bring a pan of lightly salted water to a rolling boil. Add the pasta and cook for 3 minutes only. Drain thoroughly, return to the pan and spoon over two-thirds of the pesto. Toss to coat.

3 Cut out 4 circles, about 30 cm/12 in in diameter, from non-stick baking parchment. Spoon the pasta on to one half of each circle. Top each pile of pasta with 2 prawns, 3 scallops and a few squid rings. Spoon 1 table-spoon of wine over each serving, then drizzle with the remaining coriander pesto and top with a slice of lemon.

4 Close the parcels by folding over the other half of the paper, to make a semi-circle, then turn and twist the edges of the paper to secure.

5 Place the parcels on a baking tray and bake in the preheated oven for 15 minutes, or until cooked. Serve the parcels immediately, allowing each person to open their own.

## Helpful Hint

Prepare whole squid by firmly pulling the pouch and tentacles apart. Remove the transparent quill from the pouch and discard. Rinse the pouch under cold running water, then peel off the dark skin and discard. Slice the pouch and tentacles into rings.

### INGREDIENTS
*Serves 4*

300 g/11 oz pappardelle or
  tagliatelle
8 raw tiger prawns, shelled
12 raw queen scallops
225 g/8oz baby squid, cleaned
  and cut into rings
4 tbsp dry white wine
4 thin slices of lemon

### CORIANDER PESTO:
50 g/2 oz fresh coriander leaves
1 garlic clove, peeled
25 g/1 oz pine nuts, toasted
1 tsp lemon juice
5 tbsp olive oil
1 tbsp grated Parmesan cheese
salt and freshly ground black
  pepper

# Pasta & Mussels in Tomato & Wine Sauce

1 Scrub the mussels and remove any beards. Discard any that do not close when lightly tapped. Place in a large pan with the bay leaf and pour in the wine. Cover with a tight-fitting lid and steam, shaking the pan occasionally, for 3–4 minutes, or until the mussels open. Remove the mussels with a slotted spoon, discarding any that have not opened, and reserve. Strain the cooking liquid through a muslin-lined sieve and reserve.

2 Melt the butter with the oil in a large saucepan and gently cook the onion and garlic for 10 minutes, until soft. Add the reserved cooking liquid and the tomatoes and simmer, uncovered, for 6–7 minutes, or until very soft and the sauce has reduced slightly.

3 Meanwhile, bring a large pan of lightly salted water to a rolling boil. Add the pasta and cook acording to the packet instructions, or until 'al dente'.

4 Drain the pasta thoroughly and return to the pan. Add the mussels, removing the shells if you prefer, with the tomato sauce. Stir in the basil and season to taste with salt and pepper. Toss together gently. Tip into warmed serving bowls, garnish with basil leaves and serve with crusty bread.

## INGREDIENTS
*Serves 4*

*900 g/2 lb fresh live mussels*
*1 bay leaf*
*150 ml/¼ pint light red wine*
*15 g/½ oz unsalted butter*
*1 tbsp olive oil*
*1 red onion, peeled and thinly sliced*
*2 garlic cloves, peeled and crushed*
*550 g/1¼ lb ripe tomatoes, skinned, deseeded and chopped*
*400 g/14 oz fiochetti or penne*
*3 tbsp freshly chopped or torn basil*
*salt and freshly ground black pepper*
*basil leaves, to garnish*
*crusty bread, to serve*

## Helpful Hint

Some fishmongers still sell mussels by volume rather than weight: 1.1 litres/2 pints is the equivalent of 900 g/2 lb. If you are not cooking mussels within a few hours of buying them, store in a bowl of water in a cold place or in the warmest part of the refrigerator on a hot day. Do not add salt, flour or oatmeal to the water.

# Salmon & Spaghetti in a Creamy Egg Sauce

1 Beat the eggs in a bowl with the parsley, dill, half of the Parmesan and pecorino cheeses and the white wine. Season to taste with freshly ground black pepper and reserve.

2 Bring a large pan of lightly salted water to a rolling boil. Add the spaghetti and cook according to the packet instructions, or until 'al dente'.

3 Meanwhile, cut the salmon into bite-sized pieces. Melt the butter in a large frying pan with the oil and cook the salmon pieces for 3–4 minutes, or until opaque.

4 Drain the spaghetti thoroughly, return to the pan and immediately add the egg mixture. Remove from the heat and toss well; the eggs will cook in the heat of the spaghetti to make a creamy sauce.

5 Stir in the remaining cheeses and the cooked pieces of salmon and toss again. Tip into a warmed serving bowl or on to individual plates. Garnish with sprigs of flat-leaf parsley and serve immediately.

## INGREDIENTS
### Serves 4

3 medium eggs
1 tbsp freshly chopped parsley
1 tbsp freshly chopped dill
40 g / 1½ oz freshly grated
    Parmesan cheese
40 g / 1½ oz freshly grated
    pecorino cheese
2 tbsp dry white wine
freshly ground black pepper
400 g / 14 oz spaghetti
350 g / 12 oz salmon fillet,
    skinned
25 g / 1 oz butter
1 tsp olive oil
flat-leaf parsley sprigs, to garnish

## Food Fact

This recipe is based on the classic Spaghetti alla Carbonara, which is made with smoked bacon or pancetta. Here, fresh salmon makes an equally delicious alternative. Make sure that you remove the spaghetti from the heat before adding the egg mixture and keep turning the spaghetti until the eggs cook to a light creamy sauce.

## Helpful Hint

You will not need to add salt in this recipe as the pecorino cheese is very salty.

# Creamy Coconut Seafood Pasta

**1** Bring a large pan of lightly salted water to a rolling boil. Add the pasta and cook according to the packet instructions, or until 'al dente'.

**2** Meanwhile, heat the sunflower and sesame oils together in a saucepan. Add the spring onions, garlic, chilli and ginger and cook for 3–4 minutes, or until softened.

**3** Blend the coconut milk and cream together in a jug. Add the prawns and crab meat to the pan and stir over a low heat for a few seconds to heat through.

Gradually pour in the coconut cream, stirring all the time.

**4** Stir the chopped coriander into the seafood sauce and season to taste with salt and pepper. Continue heating the sauce gently until piping hot, but do not allow to boil.

**5** Drain the pasta thoroughly and return to the pan. Add the seafood sauce and gently toss together to coat the pasta. Tip into a warmed serving dish or spoon on to individual plates. Serve immediately, garnished with fresh coriander sprigs.

## INGREDIENTS
### Serves 4

400 g/14 oz egg tagliatelle
1 tsp sunflower oil
1 tsp sesame oil
4 spring onions, trimmed and
  sliced diagonally
1 garlic clove, peeled and crushed
1 red chilli, deseeded and finely
  chopped
2.5 cm/1 inch piece fresh root
  ginger, peeled and grated
150 ml/¼ pint coconut milk
100 ml/3½ fl oz double cream
225 g/8 oz cooked peeled tiger
  prawns
185 g/6½ oz fresh white crab
  meat
2 tbsp freshly chopped coriander,
  plus sprigs to garnish
salt and freshly ground black
  pepper

## Helpful Hint

Coconut milk can be bought either in cans or long-life cartons, or you can make it yourself if you prefer. Put 125 g/4 oz desiccated coconut into a food processor or blender with 225 ml/8 fl oz boiling water and process for 30 seconds. Leave to cool for 5 minutes, then tip into a sieve lined with muslin over a bowl. Allow to drain for a few minutes, then squeeze out as much liquid as possible. Discard the coconut.

# Fettuccine with Sardines & Spinach

1 Drain the sardines and cut in half lengthwise. Remove the bones, then cut the fish into 2.5 cm/1 inch pieces and reserve.

2 Bring a large pan of lightly salted water to a rolling boil. Add the pasta and cook according to the packet instructions, or until 'al dente'.

3 Meanwhile, melt half the butter with the olive oil in a large saucepan, add the bread-crumbs and fry, stirring, until they begin to turn crisp. Add the garlic and pine nuts and continue to cook until golden-brown. Remove from the pan and reserve. Wipe the pan clean.

4 Melt the remaining butter in the pan, add the mushrooms and cook for 4–5 minutes, or until soft. Add the spinach and cook, stirring, for 1 minute, or until beginning to wilt. Stir in the crème fraîche and lemon rind and bring to the boil. Simmer gently until the spinach is just cooked. Season the sauce to taste with salt and pepper.

5 Drain the pasta thoroughly and return to the pan. Add the spinach sauce and sardine pieces and gently toss together. Tip into a warmed serving dish. Sprinkle with the toasted bread-crumbs and pine nuts and serve immediately.

## INGREDIENTS
### Serves 4

120g can sardines in olive oil
400 g/14 oz fettuccine or tagliarini
40 g/1½ oz butter
2 tbsp olive oil
50 g/2 oz one-day-old white breadcrumbs
1 garlic clove, peeled and finely chopped
50 g/2 oz pine nuts
125 g/4 oz chestnut mushrooms, wiped and sliced
125 g/4 oz baby spinach leaves, rinsed
150 ml/¼ pint crème fraîche
rind of 1 lemon, finely grated
salt and freshly ground black pepper

## Helpful Hint

Choose a full-fat crème fraîche for this recipe rather than half-fat, otherwise it may curdle. Alternatively, use soured cream if you prefer. Other canned fish such as sild or mackerel fillets may be substituted for the sardines, but check that they are in oil, and not tomato sauce, when you buy.

# Sweet-&-Sour Fish with Crispy Noodles

1 Cut the plaice fillets into 5 cm/2 inch slices. Mix the flour with the five-spice powder in a bowl. Add the fish, a few pieces at a time, and toss to coat thoroughly. Reserve.

2 Place the ginger, spring onions, sherry, soy sauce, sugar, vinegar and chilli sauce in a small saucepan and season lightly with salt and pepper. Heat gently until the sugar has dissolved, then bubble the sauce for 2–3 minutes.

3 Break the noodles into pieces about 7.5 cm/3 inch long. Heat the oil in a deep fryer to 180°C/350°F. Deep-fry small handfuls of noodles for about 30 seconds, until puffed up and crisp. Remove and drain on absorbent kitchen paper.

4 Deep-fry the plaice for 1-2 minutes, or until firm and cooked. Remove and drain on absorbent kitchen paper.

5 Place the cooked fish in a warmed serving bowl, drizzle over the sauce and garnish with spring onion tassels and slices of red chilli. Pile the noodles into another bowl and serve.

## INGREDIENTS
*Serves 4*

350 g/12 oz plaice fillets, skinned
3 tbsp plain flour
pinch of Chinese five-spice powder
2.5 cm/1 inch piece fresh root ginger, peeled and grated
4 spring onions, trimmed and finely sliced
3 tbsp dry sherry
1 tbsp dark soy sauce
2 tsp soft light brown sugar
1 tsp rice or sherry vinegar
1 tsp chilli sauce
salt and freshly ground black pepper
125 g/4 oz thin, transparent rice noodles or rice sticks
oil for deep frying

*TO GARNISH:*
spring onion tassels
slices of red chilli

## Food Fact

Chinese five-spice powder adds a taste not unlike liquorice to this dish. It is made from a mixture of Szechuan pepper, cloves, cassia, fennel and star anise, ground together to make a golden-brown powder. Add just a tiny pinch, as it has a powerful flavour.

# Warm Swordfish Niçoise

1 Place the swordfish steaks in a shallow dish. Mix the lime juice with the oil, season to taste with salt and pepper and spoon over the steaks. Turn the steaks to coat them evenly. Cover and place in the refrigerator to marinate for 1 hour.

2 Bring a large pan of lightly salted water to a rolling boil. Add the farfalle and cook according to the packet instructions, or until 'al dente'. Add the French beans about 4 minutes before the end of cooking time.

3 Mix the mustard, vinegar and sugar together in a small jug. Gradually whisk in the olive oil to make a thick dressing.

4 Cook the swordfish in a griddle pan or under a hot preheated grill for 2 minutes on each side, or until just cooked through; overcooking will make it tough and dry. Remove and cut into 2 cm/¾ inch chunks.

5 Drain the pasta and beans thoroughly and place in a large bowl. Pour over the dressing and toss to coat. Add the cooked swordfish, tomatoes, olives, hard-boiled eggs and anchovy fillets. Gently toss together, taking care not to break up the eggs.

6 Tip into a warmed serving bowl or divide the pasta between individual plates. Serve immediately.

## Helpful Hint

This dish can also be made with fresh tuna fish steaks. Prepare and cook in exactly the same way as the swordfish, although tuna can be served slightly rare, if wished. Do not marinate the fish for more than the time suggested, or it may become over-tenderised and lose its firm texture.

## INGREDIENTS
### Serves 4

4 swordfish steaks, about 2.5 cm/1 inch thick, weighing about 175 g/6 oz each

juice of 1 lime

2 tbsp olive oil

salt and freshly ground black pepper

400 g/14 oz farfalle

225 g/8 oz French beans, topped and cut in half

1 tsp Dijon mustard

2 tsp white wine vinegar

pinch caster sugar

3 tbsp olive oil

225 g/8 oz ripe tomatoes, quartered

50 g/2 oz pitted black olives

2 medium eggs, hard boiled and quartered

8 anchovy fillets, drained and cut in half lengthways

# Spaghetti Bolognese

1 Heat the olive oil in a large heavy-based pan, add the bacon and cook for 5 minutes or until slightly coloured. Add the onion, carrot, celery, garlic and bay leaf and cook, stirring, for 8 minutes, or until the vegetables are soft.

2 Add the minced beef to the pan and cook, stirring with a wooden spoon to break up any lumps in the meat, for 5-8 minutes, or until browned.

3 Stir the tomatoes and tomato paste into the mince and pour in the wine and stock. Bring to the boil, lower the heat and simmer for a least 40 minutes, stirring occasionally. The longer you leave the sauce to cook, the more intense the flavour. Season to taste with salt and pepper and remove the bay leaf.

4 Meanwhile, bring a large pan of lightly salted water to a rolling boil, add the spaghetti and cook for about 8 minutes or until 'al dente'. Drain and arrange on warmed serving plates. Top with the prepared Bolognese sauce and serve immediately sprinkled with grated Parmesan cheese.

## INGREDIENTS
### Serves 4

3 tbsp olive oil

50 g/2 oz unsmoked streaky bacon, rind removed and chopped

1 small onion, peeled and finely chopped

1 carrot, peeled and finely chopped

1 celery, trimmed and finely chopped

2 garlic cloves, peeled and crushed

1 bay leaf

500 g/1 lb 2 oz minced beef steak

400 g can chopped tomatoes

2 tbsp tomato paste

150 ml/¼ pint red wine

150 ml/¼ pint beef stock

salt and freshly gound black pepper

450 g/1 lb spaghetti

freshly grated Parmesan cheese, to serve

## Food Fact

Bolognaise sauce or *ragù alla Bolognaise*, as it is known in Italy, is enjoyed throughout the world, especially in the United States and Britain. It originated in the city of Bologna in Emilia-Romagna, where it is always served with tagliatelle, rather than spaghetti.

# Lasagne

1 Preheat the oven to 200°C/ 400°F/Gas Mark 6, 15 minutes before cooking. Melt the butter in a small heavy-based pan, add the flour and cook gently, stirring, for 2 minutes. Remove from the heat and gradually stir in the milk. Return to the heat and cook, stirring, for 2 minutes, or until the sauce thickens. Bring to the boil, remove from the heat and stir in the mustard. Season to taste with salt, pepper and nutmeg.

2 Butter a rectangular ovenproof dish and spread a thin layer of the white sauce over the base. Cover completely with 3 sheets of lasagne.

3 Spoon a quarter of the prepared Bolognese sauce over the lasagne. Spoon over a quarter of the remaining white sauce, then sprinkle with a quarter of the grated Parmesan cheese. Repeat the layers, finishing with Parmesan cheese.

4 Bake in the preheated oven for 30 minutes, or until golden-brown. Garnish with chopped parsley and serve immediately with warm garlic bread.

## INGREDIENTS
*Serves 4*

*75 g/3 oz butter*
*4 tbsp plain flour*
*750 ml/1¼ pints milk*
*1 tsp wholegrain mustard*
*salt and freshly ground black*
  *pepper*
*¼ tsp freshly grated nutmeg*
*9 sheets lasagne*
*1 quantity of prepared Bolognese*
  *sauce, see page 96*
*75g/3oz freshly grated Parmesan*
  *cheese*
*freshly chopped parsley, to garnish*
*garlic bread, to serve*

## Helpful Hint

For a change use lasagne verdi – it is green lasagne made with spinach. The shape varies according to the manufacturer and may be flat or wavy. Some have crimped edges, which help to trap the sauce and stop it running to the bottom of the dish.
  As brands come in slightly different sizes, it is worth trying several until you find the one that fits your lasagne dish perfectly!

# Cannelloni with Spicy Bolognese Filling

1 Preheat the oven to 200°C/ 400°F/Gas Mark 6, 15 minutes before cooking the stuffed cannelloni. To make the Bolognese sauce, heat the oil in a large heavy-based pan, add the onion and garlic and cook for 8 minutes, or until soft. Add the minced beef and cook, stirring with a wooden spoon to break up lumps, for 5–8 minutes, or until the meat is browned.

2 Stir in the chilli flakes, fennel seeds, oregano, tomatoes and tomato paste and pour in the wine. Season well with salt and pepper. Bring to the boil, cover and lower the heat, then simmer for at least 30 minutes, stirring occasionally. Remove the lid and simmer for a further 10 minutes. Allow to cool slightly.

3 Using a teaspoon, fill the cannelloni tubes with the meat filling. Lay the stuffed cannelloni side by side in a lightly oiled ovenproof dish.

4 Mix the double cream with three-quarters of the Parmesan cheese and the nutmeg. Pour over the cannelloni and sprinkle with the remaining cheese. Bake in the preheated oven for 30 minutes, or until golden-brown and bubbling. Serve immediately with a green salad.

## Helpful Hint

The bolognese filling can be made with all beef mince, as here, or more traditionally with a mixture of half beef and half lean minced pork. Minced chicken or turkey also work well in this recipe, although the colour is paler and the flavour less rich, but you can compensate for this by slightly increasing the quantity of herbs and spices.

### INGREDIENTS
*Serves 6*

*12 dried cannelloni tubes*
*300 ml/½ pint double cream*
*75 g/3 oz freshly grated
    Parmesan cheese*
*¼ tsp freshly grated nutmeg*
*crisp green salad, to serve*

### SPICY BOLOGNESE
    FILLING:
*2 tbsp olive oil*
*1 small onion, peeled and finely
    chopped*
*2 garlic cloves, peeled and crushed*
*500 g/1 lb 2 oz minced
    beef steak*
*¼ tsp crushed chilli flakes*
*1 tsp fennel seeds*
*2 tbsp freshly chopped oregano*
*400 g can chopped tomatoes*
*1 tbsp sun-dried tomato paste*
*150 ml/¼ pint red wine*
*salt and freshly ground black
    pepper*

# Spaghetti & Meatballs

1 Preheat the oven to 200°C/ 400°F/Gas Mark 6, 15 minutes before using. Place the chopped tomatoes, tomato paste, chilli sauce and sugar in a saucepan. Season to taste with salt and pepper and bring to the boil. Cover and simmer for 15 minutes, then cook, uncovered, for a further 10 minutes, or until the sauce has reduced and thickened.

2 Meanwhile, make the meatballs. Place the meat, breadcrumbs and onion in a food processor. Blend until all the ingredients are well mixed. Add the beaten egg, tomato paste, parsley and oregano and season to taste. Blend again.

3 Shape the mixture into small balls, about the size of an apricot, and place on an oiled baking tray. Cook in the pre-heated oven for 25–30 minutes, or until browned and cooked.

4 Meanwhile, bring a large pan of lightly salted water to a rolling boil. Add the pasta and cook according to the packet instructions, or until 'al dente'.

5 Drain the pasta and return to the pan. Pour over the tomato sauce and toss gently to coat the spaghetti. Tip into a warmed serving dish and top with the meatballs. Garnish with chopped parsley and serve immediately with grated cheese.

## INGREDIENTS
### Serves 4

400 g can chopped tomatoes
1 tbsp tomato paste
1 tsp chilli sauce
¼ tsp brown sugar
salt and freshly ground black
  pepper
350 g/12 oz spaghetti
75g/3 oz Cheddar cheese, grated,
  plus extra to serve
freshly chopped parsley, to garnish

## FOR THE MEATBALLS:

450 g/1 lb lean pork or beef
  mince
125 g/4 oz fresh breadcrumbs
1 large onion, peeled and finely
  chopped
1 medium egg, beaten
1 tbsp tomato paste
2 tbsp freshly chopped parsley
1 tbsp freshly chopped oregano

## Tasty Tip

For a crisper outside to the meatballs, you can fry them instead of baking. Heat 2 tablespoons of olive oil in a very large frying pan and cook over a medium heat for about 15 minutes, turning occasionally, until well-browned.

# Chorizo with Pasta in a Tomato Sauce

1 Melt the butter with the olive oil in a large heavy-based pan. Add the onions and sugar and cook over a very low heat, stirring occasionally, for 15 minutes, or until soft and starting to caramelize.

2 Add the garlic and chorizo to the pan and cook for 5 minutes. Stir in the chilli, chopped tomatoes and tomato paste, and pour in the wine. Season well with salt and pepper. Bring to the boil, cover, reduce the heat and simmer for 30 minutes, stirring occasionally. Remove the lid and simmer for a further 10 minutes, or until the sauce starts to thicken.

3 Meanwhile, bring a large pan of lightly salted water to a rolling boil. Add the pasta and cook according to the packet instructions, or until 'al dente'.

4 Drain the pasta, reserving 2 tablespoons of the water, and return to the pan. Add the chorizo sauce with the reserved cooking water and toss gently until the pasta is evenly covered. Tip into a warmed serving dish, sprinkle with the parsley and serve immediately.

## INGREDIENTS
*Serves 4*

*25 g/1 oz butter*
*2 tbsp olive oil*
*2 large onions, peeled and finely sliced*
*1 tsp soft brown sugar*
*2 garlic cloves, peeled and crushed*
*225 g/8 oz chorizo, sliced*
*1 chilli, deseeded and finely sliced*
*400g can chopped tomatoes*
*1 tbsp sun-dried tomato paste*
*150 ml/¼ pint red wine*
*salt and freshly ground black pepper*
*450 g/1 lb rigatoni*
*freshly chopped parsley, to garnish*

## Helpful Hint

Although there are many different types of chilli, they all have a hot, spicy flavour. Take care when preparing chillies as the volatile oils in the seeds and the membrane can cause irritation – wash your hands thoroughly afterwards.

# Moroccan Penne

1 Preheat the oven to 200° C/400°F/Gas Mark 6, 15 minutes before using. Heat the sunflower oil in a large flame-proof casserole. Add the chopped onion and fry for 5 minutes, or until softened.

2 Using a pestle and mortar, pound the garlic, coriander seeds, cumin seeds and grated nutmeg together into a paste. Add to the onion and cook for 3 minutes.

3 Add the lamb mince to the casserole and fry, stirring with a wooden spoon, for 4–5 minutes, or until the mince has broken up and browned.

4 Add the aubergine to the mince and fry for 5 minutes. Stir in the chopped tomatoes and vegetable stock and bring to the boil. Add the apricots and olives, then season well with salt and pepper. Return to the boil, lower the heat and simmer for 15 minutes.

5 Add the penne to the casserole, stir well, then cover and place in the preheated oven. Cook for 10 minutes then stir and return to the oven, uncovered, for a further 15–20 minutes, or until the pasta is 'al dente'. Remove from the oven, sprinkle with toasted pine nuts and serve immediately.

## INGREDIENTS
### Serves 4

1 tbsp sunflower oil
1 red onion, peeled and chopped
2 cloves garlic, peeled and crushed
1 tbsp coriander seeds
¼ tsp cumin seeds
¼ tsp freshly grated nutmeg
450 g/1 lb lean lamb mince
1 aubergine, trimmed and diced
400 g can chopped tomatoes
300 ml/½ pint vegetable stock
125 g/4 oz ready-to-eat apricots, chopped
12 black olives, pitted
salt and freshly ground black pepper
350 g/12 oz penne
1 tbsp toasted pine nuts, to garnish

## Helpful Hint

You can sometimes buy pine nuts ready-toasted, but if you cannot find any they are easy to toast. Sprinkle them on a foil-lined grill pan and place under a medium grill for 3–4 minutes, turning frequently until they are golden-brown. Alternatively, dry-fry them in a non-stick frying pan, tossing the nuts every few seconds. Always watch nuts when cooking them as they can burn easily.

# Spicy Chilli Beef

1 Heat the olive oil in a large heavy-based pan. Add the onion and red pepper and cook for 5 minutes, or until beginning to soften. Add the minced beef and cook over a high heat for 5–8 minutes, or until the meat is browned. Stir with a wooden spoon during cooking to break up any lumps in the meat. Add the garlic and chilli, fry for 1 minute then season to taste with salt and pepper.

2 Add the chopped tomatoes, tomato paste and the kidney beans to the pan. Bring to the boil, lower the heat, and simmer, covered, for at least 40 minutes, stirring occasionally. Stir in the grated chocolate and cook for 3 minutes, or until melted.

3 Meanwhile, bring a large pan of lightly salted water to a rolling boil. Add the fusilli and cook according to the packet instructions, or until 'al dente'.

4 Drain the pasta, return to the pan and toss with the butter and parsley. Tip into a warmed serving dish or spoon on to individual plates. Spoon the sauce over the pasta. Sprinkle with paprika and serve immediately with spoonfuls of soured cream.

## INGREDIENTS
### Serves 4

2 tbsp olive oil
1 onion, peeled and finely chopped
1 red pepper, deseeded and sliced
450 g/1 lb minced beef steak
2 garlic cloves, peeled and crushed
2 red chillies, deseeded and finely sliced
salt and freshly ground black pepper
400 g can chopped tomatoes
2 tbsp tomato paste
400 g can red kidney beans, drained
50 g/2 oz good quality, plain dark chocolate, grated
350 g/12 oz dried fusilli
knob of butter
2 tbsp freshly chopped flat-leaf parsley
paprika, to garnish
soured cream, to serve

## Food Fact

The chocolate in this traditional spicy Mexican dish adds rich warm undertones, colour and a slight sweetness, but no-one will realise it is there unless you tell them. For maximum flavour, use a good quality, plain dark chocolate with a minimum sugar content and a high percentage of cocoa solids.

# Pasta & Pork Ragù

1 Heat the sunflower oil in a large frying pan. Add the sliced leek and cook, stirring frequently, for 5 minutes, or until softened. Add the pork and cook, stirring, for 4 minutes, or until sealed.

2 Add the crushed garlic and the paprika and cayenne peppers to the pan and stir until all the pork is lightly coated in the garlic and pepper mixture.

3 Pour in the wine and 450 ml/¾ pint of the vegetable stock. Add the borlotti beans and carrots and season to taste with salt and pepper. Bring the sauce to the boil, then lower the heat and simmer for 5 minutes.

4 Meanwhile, place the egg tagliatelle in a large saucepan of lightly salted, boiling water, cover and simmer for 5 minutes, or until the pasta is cooked 'al dente'.

5 Drain the pasta, then add to the pork ragù; toss well. Adjust the seasoning, then tip into a warmed serving dish. Sprinkle with chopped parsley and serve with a little crème fraîche.

## INGREDIENTS
### Serves 4

1 tbsp sunflower oil
1 leek, trimmed and thinly sliced
225 g/8 oz pork fillet, diced
1 garlic clove, peeled and crushed
2 tsp paprika
¼ tsp cayenne pepper
150 ml/¼ pint white wine
600 ml/1 pint vegetable stock
400g can borlotti beans, drained and rinsed
2 carrots, peeled and diced
salt and freshly ground black pepper
225 g/8 oz fresh egg tagliatelle
1 tbsp freshly chopped parsley, to garnish
crème fraîche, to serve

## Helpful Hint

Pork fillet, also known as tenderloin, is a very lean and tender cut of pork. It needs little cooking time, so is perfect for this quick and simple dish. Rump or sirloin steak or boneless skinned chicken breast, cut into thin strips, could be used instead, if preferred.

# Sausage & Redcurrant Pasta Bake

1 Preheat the oven to 220°C/ 425°F/Gas Mark 7, 15 minutes before cooking. Prick the sausages, place in a shallow ovenproof dish and toss in the sunflower oil. Cook in the oven for 25–30 minutes, or until golden brown.

2 Meanwhile, melt the butter in a frying pan, add the sliced onion and fry for 5 minutes, or until golden-brown. Stir in the flour and cook for 2 minutes. Remove the pan from the heat and gradually stir in the chicken stock with the port or red wine.

3 Return the pan to the heat and bring to the boil, stirring continuously until the sauce starts to thicken. Add the thyme, bay leaf and redcurrant jelly and season well with salt and pepper. Simmer the sauce for 5 minutes.

4 Bring a large pan of salted water to a rolling boil, add the pasta and cook for about 4 minutes, or until 'al dente'. Drain thoroughly and reserve.

5 Lower the oven temperature to 200°C/400°F/Gas Mark 6. Remove the sausages from the oven, drain off any excess fat and return the sausages to the dish. Add the pasta. Pour over the sauce, removing the bay leaf, and toss together. Sprinkle with the Gruyère cheese and return to the oven for 15–20 minutes, or until bubbling and golden-brown. Serve immediately, garnished with thyme sprigs.

## Tasty Tip

For a change, try speciality sausages for this recipe. Venison or wild boar sausages would work well with the rich sauce, as would Cumberland or spicy Cambridge pork sausages.

## INGREDIENTS
### Serves 4

450 g/1 lb good quality, thick
  pork sausages
2 tsp sunflower oil
25 g/1 oz butter
1 onion, peeled and sliced
2 tbsp plain white flour
450 ml/¾ pint chicken stock
150 ml/¼ pint port or good
  quality red wine
1 tbsp freshly chopped thyme
  leaves, plus sprigs to garnish
1 bay leaf
4 tbsp redcurrant jelly
salt and freshly ground black
  pepper
350 g/12 oz fresh penne
75 g/3 oz Gruyère cheese, grated

# Pappardelle Pork with Brandy Sauce

1 Preheat the oven to 200° C/400°F/Gas Mark 6, 15 minutes before cooking. Using a sharp knife, cut two slits in each pork fillet then stuff each slit with chopped sage. Season well with salt and pepper and wrap each fillet with a slice of Parma ham.

2 Heat the olive oil in a large frying pan. Add the wrapped pork fillets and cook, turning once, for 1–2 minutes, or until the Parma ham is golden brown. Transfer to a roasting tin and cook in the preheated oven for 10–12 minutes.

3 Return the frying pan to the heat and add the brandy, scraping the bottom of the pan with a spoon to release all the flavours. Boil for 1 minute, then pour in the chicken stock. Boil for a further 2 minutes then pour in the cream and boil again for 2–3 minutes, or until the sauce has thickened slightly. Season the brandy sauce to taste.

4 Bring a large pan of lightly salted water to a rolling boil. Add the pasta and cook according to the packet instructions, or until 'al dente'. Drain the pasta thoroughly and return to the pan. Add the butter and chopped parsley and toss together. Keep the pasta warm.

5 Remove the pork from the oven and pour any juices into the brandy sauce. Pile the pasta on individual plates, season with pepper, spoon over the brandy sauce and serve immediately with the pork fillets.

## INGREDIENTS
### Serves 4

4 pork fillets, each weighing about 175 g/6 oz
1 tbsp freshly chopped sage, plus whole leaves to garnish
salt and freshly ground black pepper
4 slices Parma ham
1 tbsp olive oil
6 tbsp brandy
300 ml/½ pint chicken stock
200 ml/7 fl oz double cream
350 g/12 oz pappardelle
1–2 tsp butter
2 tbsp freshly chopped flat-leaf parsley

## Tasty Tip

An inexpensive French cooking brandy can be used for this recipe, but for a special occasion use Calvados. Made from apples, it goes particularly well with pork.

# Tagliatelle with Spicy Sausage Ragù

1 Preheat the oven to 200°C/ 400°F/Gas Mark 6, 15 minutes before cooking. Heat 1 tablespoon of the olive oil in a large frying pan. Prick the sausages, add to the pan and cook for 8–10 minutes, or until browned and cooked through. Remove and cut into thin diagonal slices. Reserve.

2 Return the pan to the heat and pour in the remaining olive oil. Add the onion and cook for 8 minutes, or until softened. Add the fennel seeds and minced pork and cook, stirring, for 5–8 minutes, or until the meat is sealed and browned.

3 Stir in the tomatoes, tomato paste and the wine or port. Season to taste with salt and pepper. Bring to the boil, cover and simmer for 30 minutes, stirring occasionally. Remove the lid and simmer for 10 minutes.

4 Bring a large pan of lightly salted water to a rolling boil. Add the pasta and cook according to the packet instructions, or until 'al dente'. Drain thoroughly and toss with the meat sauce.

5 Place half the pasta in an ovenproof dish, and cover with 4 tablespoons of the white sauce. Top with half the sausages and grated Parmesan cheese. Repeat the layering, finishing with white sauce and Parmesan cheese. Bake in the preheated oven for 20 minutes, until golden-brown. Serve immediately.

## INGREDIENTS
### Serves 4

3 tbsp olive oil

6 spicy sausages

1 small onion, peeled and finely chopped

1 tsp fennel seeds

175 g/6 oz fresh pork mince

225 g can chopped tomatoes with garlic

1 tbsp sun-dried tomato paste

2 tbsp red wine or port

salt and freshly ground black pepper

350 g/12 oz tagliatelle

300 ml/½ pint prepared white sauce, see page 98

50 g/2 oz freshly grated Parmesan cheese

## Helpful Hint

Most supermarkets sell cans of chopped tomatoes with added flavouring; if you cannot find them, simply add a large crushed garlic clove to ordinary canned tomatoes.

## Food Fact

The sweet aniseed flavour of fennel seeds has an affinity with the slight acidity of tomatoes.

# Pasta with Beef, Capers & Olives

**1** Heat the olive oil in a large frying pan over a high heat. Add the steak and cook, stirring, for 3–4 minutes, or until browned. Remove from the pan using a slotted spoon and reserve.

**2** Lower the heat, add the spring onions and garlic to the pan and cook for 1 minute. Add the courgettes and pepper and cook for 3–4 minutes.

**3** Add the oregano, capers and olives to the pan with the chopped tomatoes. Season to taste with salt and pepper, then simmer for 7 minutes, stirring

occasionally. Return the beef to the pan and simmer for 3–5 minutes, or until the sauce has thickened slightly.

**4** Meanwhile, bring a large pan of lightly salted water to a rolling boil. Add the pasta and cook according to the packet instructions, or until 'al dente'.

**5** Drain the pasta thoroughly. Return to the pan and add the beef sauce. Toss gently until the pasta is lightly coated. Tip into a warmed serving dish or on to individual plates. Sprinkle with chopped parsley and serve immediately.

## INGREDIENTS
### Serves 4

2 tbsp olive oil

300 g/11 oz rump steak, trimmed and cut into strips

4 spring onions, trimmed and sliced

2 garlic cloves, peeled and chopped

2 courgettes, trimmed and cut into strips

1 red pepper, deseeded and cut into strips

2 tsp freshly chopped oregano

2 tbsp capers, drained and rinsed

4 tbsp pitted black olives, sliced

400 g can chopped tomatoes

salt and freshly ground black pepper

450 g/1 lb fettuccine

1 tbsp freshly chopped parsley, to garnish

## Tasty Tip

When cooking the beef, it is important that it fries rather than steams in the pan, giving a beautifully brown and caramelised outside while keeping the middle moist and tender. Make sure that the oil in the pan is hot so that the strips of beef sizzle when added. Pat the beef dry with absorbent kitchen paper and cook it in two batches, so there is plenty of room to move it around the pan. Tip the first batch on to a plate and reserve while cooking the second, then return to the pan with any juices.

# Gnocchi & Parma Ham Bake

**1** Heat the oven to 180° C /350°F/Gas Mark 4, 10 minutes before cooking. Heat 2 tablespoons of the olive oil in a large frying pan and cook the onion and garlic for 5 minutes, or until softened. Stir in the tomatoes, sun-dried tomato paste and mascarpone cheese. Season to taste with salt and pepper. Add half the tarragon. Bring to the boil, then lower the heat immediately and simmer for 5 minutes.

**2** Meanwhile, bring 1.7 litres/3 pints water to the boil in a large pan. Add the remaining olive oil and a good pinch of salt. Add the gnocchi and cook for 1–2 minutes, or until they rise to the surface.

**3** Drain the gnocchi thoroughly and transfer to a large ovenproof dish. Add the tomato sauce and toss gently to coat the pasta. Combine the Cheddar or Parmesan cheese with the breadcrumbs and remaining tarragon and scatter over the pasta mixture. Top with the Parma ham and olives and season again.

**4** Cook in the preheated oven for 20–25 minutes, or until golden and bubbling. Serve immediately, garnished with parsley sprigs.

## INGREDIENTS
### Serves 4

3 tbsp olive oil
1 red onion, peeled and sliced
2 garlic cloves, peeled
175 g/6 oz plum tomatoes, skinned and quartered
2 tbsp sun-dried tomato paste
250 g tub mascarpone cheese
salt and freshly ground black pepper
1 tbsp freshly chopped tarragon
300 g/11 oz fresh gnocchi
125 g/4 oz Cheddar or Parmesan cheese, grated
50 g/2 oz fresh white breadcrumbs
50 g/2 oz Parma ham, sliced
10 pitted green olives, halved
sprigs of flat-leaf parsley. to garnish

## Helpful Hint

Make sure that you buy gnocchi potato dumplings for this recipe and not gnocchi sardi, a pasta of the same name. It is important to use a large pan of boiling water so that the gnocchi have plenty of room to move around, otherwise they would stick together during cooking. If you do not have a large enough pan, cook the gnocchi in two batches.

# Chinese Beef with Angel Hair Pasta

**1** Crush the peppercorns, using a pestle and mortar. Transfer to a shallow bowl and combine with the chilli powder, Szechuan pepper, light soy sauce and sherry. Add the beef strips and stir until lightly coated. Cover and place in the refrigerator to marinate for 3 hours; stir occasionally during this time.

**2** When ready to cook, bring a large pan of lightly salted water to a rolling boil. Add the pasta and cook according to the packet instructions, or until 'al dente'. Drain thoroughly and return to the pan. Add the sesame oil and toss lightly. Keep the pasta warm.

**3** Heat a wok or large frying pan, add the sunflower oil and heat until very hot. Add the shredded spring onions with the sliced red and green peppers and stir-fry for 2 minutes.

**4** Drain the beef, reserving the marinade, then add the beef to the wok or pan and stir-fry for 3 minutes. Pour the marinade and stir-fry for 1-2 minutes, until the steak is tender.

**5** Pile the pasta on to 4 warmed plates. Top with the stir-fried beef and peppers and garnish with toasted sesame seeds and shredded spring onions. Serve immediately.

## Food Fact

Szechuan pepper, which is also known as Sichuan pepper, anise pepper and *fagara*, is not related in any way to black and white pepper. It is the reddish-brown dried berry of the Chinese prickly ash tree and has a pronounced spicy, woody flavour. It is one of the essential ingredients of Chinese five-spice powder.

### INGREDIENTS
*Serves 4*

1 tbsp pink peppercorns
1 tbsp chilli powder
1 tbsp Szechuan pepper
3 tbsp light soy sauce
3 tbsp dry sherry
450 g/1 lb sirloin steak, cut into strips
350 g/12 oz angel hair pasta
1 tbsp sesame oil
1 tbsp sunflower oil
1 bunch spring onions, trimmed and finely shredded, plus extra to garnish
1 red pepper, deseeded and thinly sliced
1 green pepper, deseeded and thinly sliced
1 tbsp toasted sesame seeds, to garnish

# Lamb Arrabbiata

1 Heat 2 tablespoons of the olive oil in a large frying pan and cook the lamb for 5–7 minutes, or until sealed. Remove from the pan using a slotted spoon and reserve.

2 Heat the remaining oil in the pan, add the onion, garlic and chilli and cook until softened. Add the tomatoes, bring to the boil, then simmer for 10 minutes.

3 Return the browned lamb to the pan with the olives and pour in the wine. Bring the sauce back to the boil, reduce the heat then simmer, uncovered, for 15 minutes, until the lamb is tender. Season to taste with salt and pepper.

4 Meanwhile, bring a large pan of lightly salted water to a rolling boil. Add the pasta and cook according to the packet instructions, or until 'al dente'.

5 Drain the pasta, toss in the butter, then add to the sauce and mix lightly. Stir in 4 table-spoons of the chopped parsley, then tip into a warmed serving dish. Sprinkle with the remaining parsley and serve immediately.

## INGREDIENTS
*Serves 4*

4 tbsp olive oil

450 g/1 lb lamb fillets, cubed

1 large onion, peeled and sliced

4 garlic cloves, peeled and finely chopped

1 red chilli, deseeded and finely chopped

400 g can chopped tomatoes

175 g/6 oz pitted black olives, halved

150 ml/¼ pint white wine

salt and freshly ground black pepper

275 g/10 oz farfalle pasta

1 tsp butter

4 tbsp freshly chopped parsley, plus 1 tbsp to garnish

## Food Fact

When cooking pasta, remember to use a very large saucepan so that the pasta has plenty of time to move around freely. Once the water has come to the boil, add the pasta, stir, cover with a lid and return to the boil. The lid can then be removed so that the water does not boil over.

## Helpful Hint

Lamb fillet can be quite fatty – cut off and discard as much fat as possible. If preferred leg of lamb can be used instead.

# Creamed Lamb & Wild Mushroom Pasta

**1** Place the porcini in a small bowl and cover with almost boiling water. Leave to soak for 30 minutes. Drain the porcini, reserving the soaking liquid. Chop the porcini finely.

**2** Bring a large pan of lightly salted water to a rolling boil. Add the pasta and cook according to the packet instructions, or until 'al dente'.

**3** Meanwhile, melt the butter with the olive oil in a large frying pan and fry the lamb to seal. Add the garlic, mushrooms and prepared porcini and cook for 5 minutes, or until just soft.

**4** Add the wine and the reserved porcini soaking liquid, then simmer for 2 minutes. Stir in the cream with the sesasoning and simmer for 1–2 minutes, or until just thickened.

**5** Drain the pasta thoroughly, reserving about 4 tablespoons of the cooking water. Return the pasta to the pan. Pour over the mushroom sauce and toss lightly together, adding the pasta water if the sauce is too thick. Tip into a warmed serving dish or spoon on to individual plates. Garnish with the chopped parsley and serve immediately with grated Parmesan cheese.

## Helpful Hint

Dried porcini mushrooms have a rich, intense flavour. After soaking, they should be briefly rinsed to remove any grit or dirt. Strain the soaking liquid through muslin or a very fine sieve. If you do not have either of these, leave it to settle for about 10 minutes; grit will sink to the bottom and the liquid can be poured off, leaving any sediment behind.

### INGREDIENTS
*Serves 4*

25 g/1 oz dried porcini

450 g/1 lb pasta shapes

25g/1 oz butter

1 tbsp olive oil

350 g/12 oz lamb neck fillet, thinly sliced

1 garlic clove, peeled and crushed

225 g/8 oz brown or wild mushrooms, wiped and sliced

4 tbsp white wine

125 ml/4 fl oz double cream

salt and freshly ground black pepper

1 tbsp freshly chopped parsley, to garnish

freshly grated Parmesan cheese, to serve

# Tagliatelle with Creamy Liver & Basil

1 Season the flour lightly with salt and pepper and place in a large plastic bag. Add the liver and toss gently to coat. Remove the liver from the bag and reserve.

2 Melt the butter with the olive oil in a large frying pan. Add the onion and garlic and fry for 6–8 minutes, or until the onions begin to colour. Add the liver and fry until brown on all sides.

3 Stir in the chicken stock, tomato paste and sun-dried tomatoes. Bring to the boil, reduce the heat and simmer very gently for 10 minutes.

4 Meanwhile, bring a large pan of lightly salted water to a rolling boil. Add the pasta and cook according to the packet instructions, or until 'al dente'.

5 Stir the chopped basil and cream into the liver sauce and season to taste.

6 Drain the pasta thoroughly, reserving 2 tablespoons of the cooking water. Tip the pasta into a warmed serving dish or pile on to individual plates. Stir the reserved cooking water into the liver sauce and pour over the pasta. Toss lightly to coat the pasta. Garnish with basil leaves and serve immediately.

## Helpful Hint

Although not as delicately flavoured as calves' liver, lamb's liver can be wonderfully tender and moist if gently simmered, as here. To tone down the flavour, it can be soaked in a little milk for 1 hour after preparation. Drain the liver and pat it dry on absorbent kitchen paper before cooking.

### INGREDIENTS
*Serves 4*

*25 g/1 oz plain flour*
*salt and freshly ground black pepper*
*450 g/1 lb lamb's liver, thinly sliced and cut into bite-sized pieces*
*25 g/1 oz butter*
*1 tbsp olive oil*
*2 red onions, peeled and sliced*
*1 garlic clove, peeled and sliced*
*150 ml/¼ pint chicken stock*
*1 tbsp tomato paste*
*2 sun-dried tomatoes, finely chopped*
*1 tbsp freshly chopped basil*
*150 ml/¼ pint double cream*
*350 g/12 oz tagliatelle verdi*
*fresh basil leaves, to garnish*

# Gammon with Red Wine Sauce & Pasta

1 Preheat the grill to a medium heat before cooking. Heat the butter with the red wine in a large heavy-based pan. Add the onions, cover with a tight fitting lid and cook over a very low heat for 30 minutes, or until softened and transparent. Remove the lid from the pan, stir in the orange juice and sugar, then increase the heat and cook for about 10 minutes, until the onions are golden.

2 Meanwhile cook the gammon steak under the preheated grill, turning at least once, for 4–6 minutes, or until tender. Cut the cooked gammon into bite-sized pieces. Reserve and keep warm.

3 Meanwhile, bring a large pan of very lightly salted water to a rolling boil. Add the pasta and cook according to the packet instructions, or until 'al dente'. Drain the pasta thoroughly, return to the pan, season with a little pepper and keep warm.

4 Stir the wholegrain mustard and chopped parsley into the onion sauce then pour over the pasta. Add the gammon pieces to the pan and toss lightly to thoroughly coat the pasta with the sauce. Pile the pasta mixture on to 2 warmed serving plates. Garnish with sprigs of flat-leaf parsley and serve immediately.

## INGREDIENTS
*Serves 2*

*25 g/1 oz butter*
*150 ml/¼ pint red wine*
*4 red onions, peeled and sliced*
*4 tbsp orange juice*
*1 tsp soft brown sugar*
*225 g/8 oz gammon steak, trimmed*
*freshly ground black pepper*
*175 g/6 oz fusilli*
*3 tbsp wholegrain mustard*
*2 tbsp freshly chopped flat-leaf parsley, plus sprigs to garnish*

## Helpful Hint

Gammon can be slightly salty, so add only a little salt when cooking the pasta. Wholegrain mustard, sometimes labelled Meaux mustard, is made from mixed mustard seeds. This gives it a grainy texture and a fruity, spicy flavour that goes particularly well with gammon.

# Prosciutto & Gruyère Carbonara

1 Place the egg yolks with 6 tablespoons of the Gruyère cheese in a bowl and mix lightly until well blended, then reserve.

2 Heat the olive oil in a large pan and cook the garlic and shallots for 5 minutes, or until golden-brown. Add the prosciutto ham, then cook for a further 1 minute. Pour in the dry vermouth and simmer for 2 minutes, then remove from the heat. Season to taste with salt and pepper and keep warm.

3 Meanwhile, bring a large pan of lightly salted water to a rolling boil. Add the pasta and cook according to the packet instructions, or until 'al dente'. Drain thoroughly, reserving 4 tablespoons of the water, and return the pasta to the pan.

4 Remove from the heat, then add the egg and cheese mixture with the butter to the pasta; toss lightly until coated. Add the prosciutto mixture and toss again, adding the reserved pasta water, if needed, to moisten. Season to taste and sprinkle with the remaining Gruyère cheese and the shredded basil leaves. Garnish with basil sprigs and serve immediately.

## INGREDIENTS
### Serves 4

3 medium egg yolks
50 g/2 oz Gruyère cheese, grated
2 tbsp olive oil
2 garlic cloves, peeled and crushed
2 shallots, peeled and finely
  chopped
200 g/7 oz prosciutto ham, cut
  into strips
4 tbsp dry vermouth
salt and freshly ground black
  pepper
450 g/1 lb spaghetti
15 g/½ oz butter
1 tbsp freshly shredded basil leaves
basil sprigs, to garnish

## Food Fact

Gruyère cheese is now produced in many countries, including the United States and France. It is named after the Swiss mountain village where it originated and is still made. The pale yellow cheese is pitted with pea-sized holes and has a firm texture and a sweet, slightly nutty taste.

# Gnocchi with Tuscan Beef Ragù

1 Preheat the oven to 200°C/ 400°F/Gas Mark 6, 15 minutes before cooking. Place the porcini in a small bowl and cover with almost boiling water. Leave to soak for 30 minutes. Drain, reserving the soaking liquid and straining it through a muslin-lined sieve. Chop the porcini.

2 Heat the olive oil in a large heavy-based pan. Add the onion, carrot, celery, fennel and garlic and cook for 8 minutes, stirring, or until soft. Add the minced steak and cook, stirring, for 5–8 minutes, or until sealed and any lumps are broken up.

3 Pour in the wine, then add the porcini with half the pine nuts, the rosemary and tomato paste. Stir in the porcini soaking liquid then simmer for 5 minutes. Add the chopped tomatoes and simmer gently for about 40 minutes, stirring occasionally.

4 Meanwhile, bring 1.7 litres/ 3 pints of lightly salted water to a rolling boil in a large pan. Add the gnocchi and cook for 1–2 minutes, until they rise to the surface.

5 Drain the gnocchi and place in an ovenproof dish. Stir in three-quarters of the mozzarella cheese with the beef sauce. Top with the remaining mozzarella and pine nuts, then bake in the preheated oven for 20 minutes, until golden-brown. Serve immediately.

## INGREDIENTS
### Serves 4

25 g/1 oz dried porcini
3 tbsp olive oil
1 small onion, peeled and finely chopped
1 carrot, peeled and finely chopped
1 celery, trimmed and finely chopped
1 fennel bulb, trimmed and sliced
2 garlic cloves, peeled and crushed
450 g/1 lb fresh beef steak mince
4 tbsp red wine
50 g/2 oz pine nuts
1 tbsp freshly chopped rosemary
2 tbsp tomato paste
400 g can chopped tomatoes
225 g/8 oz fresh gnocchi
salt and freshly ground black pepper
100 g/4 oz mozzarella cheese, cubed

## Food Fact

Pine nuts are small, creamy-coloured, tear-shaped nuts from the base of the cone scales of the Mediterranean stone pine. They may become rancid if kept too long, due to their high oil content, so buy in small quantities and use within 1–2 months.

# Hot Duck Pasta Salad

1 Preheat the oven to 200°C/ 400°F/Gas Mark 6. Place the duck breasts on a baking tray lined with tinfoil. Mix together the wholegrain mustard and honey, season lightly with salt and pepper then spread over the duck breasts. Roast in the pre-heated oven for 20–30 minutes, or until tender. Remove from the oven and keep warm.

2 Meanwhile, place the eggs in a small saucepan, cover with water and bring to the boil. Simmer for 8 minutes, then drain. Bring a large pan of lightly salted water to a rolling boil. Add the beans and pasta, return to the boil and cook according to the packet instructions, or until 'al dente'. Drain the pasta and beans and refresh under cold running water.

3 Place the pasta and beans in a bowl, add the carrot, sweetcorn and spinach leaves and toss lightly. Shell the eggs, cut into wedges and arrange on top of the pasta. Slice the duck breasts then place them on top of the salad. Beat the dressing ingredients together in a bowl until well blended, then drizzle over the salad. Serve immediately.

## Helpful Hint

Eggs should never be boiled rapidly as this may cause the shells to crack and make the egg white rubbery. When cooking hard-boiled eggs for salads, turn the eggs gently once or twice in the first few minutes of cooking, so that the yolks stay in the middle. As soon as the eggs are cooked, remove them from the pan and place in a bowl of very cold water to prevent dark rings forming around the yolk.

## INGREDIENTS
### Serves 6

3 boneless and skinless duck breasts
1 tbsp wholegrain mustard
1 tbsp clear honey
salt and freshly ground black pepper
4 medium eggs
450 g/1 lb fusilli
125 g/4 oz French beans, trimmed
1 large carrot, peeled and cut into thin batons
125 g/4 oz sweetcorn kernels, cooked if frozen
75 g/3 oz fresh baby spinach leaves, shredded

### FOR THE DRESSING:
8 tbsp French dressing
1 tsp horseradish sauce
4 tbsp crème fraîche

# Chicken Tagliatelle

1 Bring a large pan of lightly salted water to a rolling boil. Add the pasta and cook according to the packet instructions, or until 'al dente'. Add the peas to the pan 5 minutes before the end of cooking time and cook until tender. Drain the pasta and peas, return to the pan and keep warm.

2 Trim the chicken if necessary, then cut into bite-sized pieces. Heat the olive oil in a large frying pan, add the chicken and cook for 8 minutes, or until golden, stirring occasionally.

3 Add the cucumber and cook for 2 minutes, or until slightly softened, stirring occasionally. Stir in the vermouth, bring to the boil, then lower the heat and simmer for 3 minutes, or until reduced slightly.

4 Add the cream to the pan, bring to the boil, stirring constantly, then stir in the Stilton cheese and snipped chives. Season to taste with salt and pepper. Heat through thoroughly, stirring occasionally, until the cheese is just beginning to melt.

5 Toss the chicken mixture into the pasta. Tip into a warmed serving dish or on to individual plates. Garnish and serve immediately.

## INGREDIENTS
### Serves 4

350 g/12 oz tagliatelle
125 g/4 oz frozen peas
4 boneless and skinless chicken breasts
2 tbsp olive oil
¼ cucumber, cut into strips
150 ml/¼ pint dry vermouth
150 ml/¼ pint double cream
125 g/4 oz Stilton cheese, crumbled
3 tbsp freshly snipped chives, plus extra to garnish
salt and freshly ground black pepper
fresh herbs, to garnish

## Helpful Hint

Chives add a mild onion flavour and attractive colour to this dish. If you do not have any, finely shred the green tops of spring onions and use them instead. If preferred, a mixture of dry white wine and 1–2 tablespoons of dry sherry can be substituted for the vermouth.

# Mixed Vegetable & Chicken Pasta

1 Preheat the grill just before using. Cut the chicken into thin strips. Trim the leeks, leaving some of the dark green tops, then shred and wash thoroughly in plenty of cold water. Peel the onion and cut into thin wedges.

2 Bring a large pan of lightly salted water to a rolling boil. Add the pasta and cook according to the packet instructions, or until 'al dente'.

3 Meanwhile, melt butter with the olive oil in a large heavy-based pan, add the chicken and cook, stirring occasionally, for 8 minutes, or until browned all over. Add the leeks and onion and cook for 5 minutes, or until softened. Add the garlic and cherry tomatoes and cook for a further 2 minutes.

4 Stir the cream and asparagus tips into the chicken and vegetable mixture, bring to the boil slowly, then remove from the heat. Drain the pasta thoroughly and return to the pan. Pour the sauce over the pasta, season to taste with salt and pepper, then toss lightly.

5 Tip the pasta mixture into a gratin dish and sprinkle with the cheese. Cook under the preheated grill for 5 minutes, or until bubbling and golden, turning the dish occasionally. Serve immediately with a green salad.

## INGREDIENTS
*Serves 4*

*3 boneless and skinless chicken breasts*
*2 leeks*
*1 red onion*
*350 g/12 oz pasta shells*
*25 g/1 oz butter*
*2 tbsp olive oil*
*1 garlic clove, peeled and chopped*
*175 g/6 oz cherry tomatoes, halved*
*200 ml/7 fl oz double cream*
*425 g can asparagus tips, drained*
*salt and freshly ground black pepper*
*125 g/4 oz double Gloucester cheese with chives, crumbled*
*green salad, to serve*

## Tasty Tip

Fresh asparagus is in season during May and June and can be used in place of canned. Tie in small bundles and cook in lightly salted, boiling water for 5–8 minutes.

# Herb-baked Chicken with Tagliatelle

1 Preheat the oven to 200°C/400°F/Gas Mark 6, 15 minute before cooking. Mix together the breadcrumbs, 1 tablespoon of the olive oil, the oregano and tomato paste. Season to taste with salt and pepper. Place the chicken breasts well apart in a roasting tin and coat with the breadcrumb mixture.

2 Mix the plum tomatoes with the chopped basil and white wine. Season to taste, then spoon evenly round the chicken.

3 Drizzle the remaining olive oil over the chicken breasts and cook in the preheated oven for 20–30minutes, or until the chicken is golden and the juices run clear when a skewer is inserted into the flesh.

4 Meanwhile, bring a large pan of lightly salted water to a rolling boil. Add the pasta and cook according to the packet instructions, or until 'al dente'.

5 Drain the pasta thoroughly and transfer to warmed serving plates. Arrange the chicken breasts on top of the pasta and spoon over the sauce. Garnish with sprigs of basil and serve immediately.

## INGREDIENTS
*Serves 4*

*75 g/3 oz fresh white breadcrumbs*
*3 tbsp olive oil*
*1 tsp dried oregano*
*2 tbsp sun-dried tomato paste*
*salt and freshly ground black pepper*
*4 boneless and skinless chicken breasts, each about 150 g/5 oz*
*2 x 400 g cans plum tomatoes*
*4 tbsp freshly chopped basil*
*2 tbsp dry white wine*
*350 g/12 oz tagliatelle*
*fresh basil sprigs, to garnish*

## Food Fact

Sun-dried tomatoes are ripened on the vine, then split open and dried in the sun to give a deep, concentrated caramelised flavour. Sun-dried tomato paste usually comes in glass jars, but can also be found in tubes. Once opened, store in the refrigerator and, if in a jar, cover the surface with a teaspoonful of olive oil to keep fresh.

# Creamy Chicken & Sausage Penne

**1** Heat the olive oil in a large frying pan, add the shallots and cook for 3 minutes, or until golden. Remove and drain on absorbent kitchen paper. Add the chicken thighs to the pan and cook for 5 minutes, turning frequently until browned. Drain on absorbent kitchen paper.

**2** Add the smoked sausage and chestnut mushrooms to the pan and cook for 3 minutes, or until browned. Drain separately on absorbent kitchen paper.

**3** Return the shallots, chicken and sausage to the pan, then add the garlic, paprika and thyme and cook for 1 minute, stirring. Pour in the wine and stock and season to taste with black pepper. Bring to the boil, lower the heat and simmer, covered, for 15 minutes.

**4** Add the mushrooms to the pan and simmer, covered, for 15 minutes, or until the chicken is tender.

**5** Meanwhile, bring a large pan of lightly salted water to a rolling boil. Add the penne and cook according to the packet instructions, or until 'al dente'. Drain thoroughly.

**6** Stir the mascarpone cheese into the chicken sauce and heat through, stirring gently. Spoon the pasta on to a warmed serving dish, top with the sauce, garnish and serve immediately.

## INGREDIENTS
### Serves 4

*2 tbsp olive oil*
*225 g/8 oz shallots, peeled*
*8 chicken thighs*
*175 g/6 oz smoked sausage, thickly sliced*
*125 g/4 oz chestnut mushrooms, wiped and halved*
*2 garlic cloves, peeled and chopped*
*1 tbsp paprika*
*1 small bunch fresh thyme, chopped, plus leaves to garnish*
*150 ml/¼ pint red wine*
*300 ml/½ pint chicken stock*
*freshly ground black pepper*
*350 g/12 oz penne*
*250 g carton mascarpone cheese*

## Food Fact

Mascarpone is a rich, soft white cheese, more like cream than cheese. Its slightly sweet flavour means that it is frequently used in desserts, but it also makes a wonderfully smooth quick sauce for cooked pasta as it simply melts in the heat.

# Creamy Turkey & Tomato Pasta

1 Preheat the oven to 200°C/ 400°F/Gas Mark 6. Heat 2 tablespoons of the olive oil in a large frying pan. Add the turkey and cook for 5 minutes, or until sealed, turning occasionally. Transfer to a roasting tin and add the remaining olive oil, the vine tomatoes, garlic and balsamic vinegar. Stir well and season to taste with salt and pepper. Cook in the preheated oven for 30 minutes, or until the turkey is tender, turning the tomatoes and turkey once.

2 Meanwhile, bring a large pan of lightly salted water to a rolling boil. Add the pasta and cook according to the packet instructions, or until 'al dente'. Drain, return to the pan and keep warm. Stir the basil and seasoning into the crème fraîche.

3 Remove the roasting tin from the oven and discard the vines. Stir the crème fraîche and basil mix into the turkey and tomato mixture and return to the oven for 1–2 minutes, or until thoroughly heated through.

4 Stir the turkey and tomato mixture into the pasta and toss lightly together. Tip into a warmed serving dish. Garnish with Parmesan cheese shavings and serve immediately.

## INGREDIENTS
### Serves 4

4 tbsp olive oil
450 g/1 lb turkey breasts, cut into bite-sized pieces
550 g/1¼ lb cherry tomatoes, on the vine
2 garlic cloves, peeled and chopped
4 tbsp balsamic vinegar
4 tbsp freshly chopped basil
salt and freshly ground black pepper
200 ml tub crème fraîche
350 g/12 oz tagliatelle
shaved Parmesan cheese, to garnish

## Helpful Hint

Balsamic vinegar is dark in colour with a mellow sweet and sour flavour. It is made from concentrated grape juice and fermented in wooden barrels. Like good wine, the vinegar improves and becomes darker and more syrupy the longer it is aged. Less expensive vinegars bought from supermarkets have been matured for three or four years only. The flavour is nonetheless wonderful and perfect for this recipe.

# Parma Ham-wrapped Chicken with Ribbon Pasta

1 Cut each chicken breast into 3 pieces and season well with salt and pepper. Wrap each chicken piece in a slice of Parma ham to enclose completely, securing if necessary with either fine twine or cocktail sticks.

2 Heat the oil in a large frying pan and cook the chicken, turning occasionally, for 12–15 minutes, or until thoroughly cooked. Remove from the pan with a slotted spoon and reserve.

3 Meanwhile, bring a large pan of lightly salted water to a rolling boil. Add the pasta and cook according to the packet instructions, or until 'al dente'.

4 Add the garlic and spring onions to the frying pan and cook, stirring occasionally, for 2 minutes, or until softened. Stir in the tomatoes, lemon juice and crème fraîche. Bring to the boil, lower the heat and simmer, covered, for 3 minutes. Stir in the parsley and sugar, season to taste, then return the chicken to the pan and heat for 2–3 minutes, or until piping hot.

5 Drain the pasta thoroughly and mix in the chopped parsley, then spoon on to a warmed serving dish or individual plates. Arrange the chicken and sauce over the pasta. Garnish and serve immediately.

## INGREDIENTS
### Serves 4

4 boneless and skinless chicken breasts
salt and freshly ground black pepper
12 slices Parma ham
2 tbsp olive oil
350 g/12 oz ribbon pasta
1 garlic clove, peeled and chopped
1 bunch spring onions, trimmed and diagonally sliced
400 g can chopped tomatoes
juice of 1 lemon
150 ml/¼ pint crème fraîche
3 tbsp freshly chopped parsley
pinch of sugar
freshly grated Parmesan cheese, to garnish

## Food Fact

Crème fraîche has a slightly sour taste and a thick, spoonable texture. It is made in a similar way to yogurt, by introducing a bacterial culture to cream. This produces lactic acid, which makes the cream curdle and thicken. The half-fat version is best avoided for cooking; it sometimes separates when boiled.

# Baked Aubergines with Tomato & Mozzarella

**1** Preheat the oven to 200° C/400°F/Gas Mark 6, 15 minutes before cooking. Place the aubergine slices in a colander and sprinkle with salt. Leave for 1 hour or until the juices run clear. Rinse and dry on absorbent kitchen paper.

**2** Heat 3–5 tablespoons of the olive oil in a large frying pan and cook the prepared aubergines in batches for 2 minutes on each side, or until softened. Remove and drain on absorbent kitchen paper.

**3** Heat 1 tablespoon of olive oil in a saucepan, add the turkey mince and cook for 5 minutes, or until browned and sealed.

**4** Add the onion to the pan and cook for 5 minutes, or until softened. Add the chopped garlic, the tomatoes and mixed herbs. Pour in the wine and season to taste with salt and pepper. Bring to the boil, lower the heat then simmer for 15 minutes, or until thickened.

**5** Meanwhile, bring a large pan of lightly salted water to a rolling boil. Add the macaroni and cook according to the packet instructions, or until 'al dente'. Drain thoroughly.

**6** Spoon half the tomato mixture into a lightly oiled ovenproof dish. Top with half the aubergine, pasta and chopped basil, then season lightly. Repeat the layers, finishing with a layer of aubergine. Sprinkle with the mozzarella and Parmesan cheeses, then bake in the preheated oven for 30 minutes, or until golden and bubbling. Serve immediately.

## INGREDIENTS
*Serves 4*

*3 medium aubergines, trimmed and sliced*
*salt and freshly ground black pepper*
*4–6 tbsp olive oil*
*450 g/1 lb fresh turkey mince*
*1 onion, peeled and chopped*
*2 garlic cloves, peeled and chopped*
*2 x 400 g cans cherry tomatoes*
*1 tbsp fresh mixed herbs*
*200 ml/7 fl oz red wine*
*350 g/12 oz macaroni*
*5 tbsp freshly chopped basil*
*125 g/4 oz mozzarella cheese, drained and chopped*
*50 g/2 oz freshly grated Parmesan cheese*

## Helpful Hint

Aubergines are salted to remove bitterness, although they are now less bitter. Salting also removes moisture so they absorb less oil when fried.

# Mini Chicken Balls with Tagliatelle

1 Mix the chicken and tomatoes together and season to taste with salt and pepper. Divide the mixture into 32 pieces and roll into balls. Transfer to a baking sheet, cover and leave in the refrigerator for 1 hour.

2 Melt the butter in a large frying pan, add the chicken balls and cook for 5 minutes, or until golden, turning occasionally. Remove, drain on absorbent kitchen paper and keep warm.

3 Add the leeks and broad beans to the frying pan and cook, stirring, for 10 minutes or until cooked and tender. Return the chicken balls to the pan, then stir in the cream and Parmesan cheese and heat through.

4 Meanwhile, bring a large pan of lightly salted water to a rolling boil. Add the pasta and cook according to the packet instructions, or until 'al dente'.

5 Bring a separate frying pan full of water to the boil, crack in the eggs and simmer for 2–4 minutes, or until poached to personal preference.

6 Meanwhile, drain the pasta thoroughly and return to the pan. Pour the chicken ball and vegetable sauce over the pasta, toss lightly and heat through for 1–2 minutes. Arrange on warmed individual plates and top with the poached eggs. Garnish with fresh herbs and serve immediately.

## INGREDIENTS
### Serves 4

*450 g/1 lb fresh chicken mince*
*50 g/2 oz sun-dried tomatoes, drained and finely chopped*
*salt and freshly ground black pepper*
*25 g/1 oz butter*
*1 tbsp oil*
*350 g/12 oz leeks, trimmed and diagonally sliced*
*125 g/4 oz frozen broad beans*
*300 ml/½ pint single cream*
*50 g/2 oz freshly grated Parmesan cheese*
*350 g/12 oz tagliatelle*
*4 medium eggs*
*fresh herbs, to garnish*

## Helpful Hint

Chilling the chicken balls firms them, so that they retain their shape when cooked. They need plenty of room for turning; if necessary cook in two batches, halving the butter for each. The butter must be sizzling before the meatballs are added.

# Pasta & Pepper Salad

1 Preheat the oven to 200°C/ 400°F/Gas Mark 6. Spoon the olive oil into a roasting tin and heat in the oven for 2 minutes, or until almost smoking. Remove from the oven, add the peppers, courgette and aubergine and stir until coated. Bake for 30 minutes, or until charred, stirring occasionally.

2 Bring a large pan of lightly salted water to a rolling boil. Add the pasta and cook according to the packet instructions, or until 'al dente'. Drain and refresh under cold running water. Drain thoroughly, place in a large salad bowl and reserve.

3 Remove the cooked vegetables from the oven and allow to cool. Add to the cooled pasta, together with the quartered tomatoes, chopped basil leaves, pesto, garlic and lemon juice. Toss lightly to mix.

4 Shred the chicken roughly into small pieces and stir into the pasta and vegetable mixture. Season to taste with salt and pepper, then sprinkle the crumbled feta cheese over the pasta and stir gently. Cover the dish and leave to marinate for 30 minutes, stirring occasionally. Serve the salad with fresh crusty bread.

## Helpful Hint

Use a large non-stick roasting tin for cooking the vegetables if you have one, and check and move them around frequently, so that they brown evenly. For extra flavour, use a garlic or chilli-flavoured olive oil and tuck a sprig or two of fresh herbs, such as rosemary or thyme, under the vegetables.

### INGREDIENTS
*Serves 4*

4 tbsp olive oil
1 each red, orange and yellow pepper, deseeded and cut into chunks
1 large courgette, trimmed and cut into chunks
1 medium aubergine, trimmed and diced
275 g/10 oz fusilli
4 plum tomatoes, quartered
1 bunch fresh basil leaves, roughly chopped
2 tbsp pesto
2 garlic cloves, peeled and roughly chopped
1 tbsp lemon juice
225 g/8 oz boneless and skinless roasted chicken breast
salt and freshly ground black pepper
125 g/4 oz feta cheese, crumbled
crusty bread, to serve

# Chicken Marengo

1 Season the flour with salt and pepper and toss the chicken in the flour to coat. Heat 2 tablespoons of the olive oil in a large frying pan and cook the chicken for 7 minutes, or until browned all over, turning occasionally. Remove from the pan using a slotted spoon and keep warm.

2 Add the remaining oil to the pan, add the onion and cook, stirring occasionally, for 5 minutes, or until softened and starting to brown. Add the garlic, tomatoes, tomato paste, basil and thyme. Pour in the wine or chicken stock and season well. Bring to the boil.

Stir in the chicken pieces and simmer for 15 minutes, or until the chicken is tender and the sauce has thickened.

3 Meanwhile, bring a large pan of lightly salted water to a rolling boil. Add the rigatoni and cook according to the packet instructions, or until 'al dente'.

4 Drain the rigatoni thoroughly, return to the pan and stir in the chopped parsley. Tip the pasta into a warmed large serving dish or spoon on to individual plates. Spoon over the chicken sauce and serve immediately.

## INGREDIENTS
### Serves 4

2 tbsp plain flour
salt and freshly ground black pepper
4 boneless and skinless chicken breasts, cut into bite-sized pieces
4 tbsp olive oil
1 Spanish onion, peeled and chopped
1 garlic clove, peeled and chopped
400 g can chopped tomatoes
2 tbsp sun-dried tomato paste
3 tbsp freshly chopped basil
3 tbsp freshly chopped thyme
125 ml/4 fl oz dry white wine or chicken stock
350 g/12 oz rigatoni
3 tbsp freshly chopped flat-leaf parsley

## Helpful Hint

Spanish onions have a milder flavour and tend to be larger than English ones. Cook the onion over a fairly low heat until really soft, stirring frequently towards the end to stop it sticking. Let it caramelise and brown very slightly as this adds a richer flavour and golden colour to the final dish.

# Turkey & Oven-roasted Vegetable Salad

1 Preheat the oven to 200°C/ 400°F/Gas Mark 6, 15 minutes before cooking. Line a large roasting tin with tinfoil, pour in half the olive oil and place in the oven for 3 minutes, or until very hot. Remove from the oven, add the courgettes and peppers and stir until evenly coated. Bake for 30–35 minutes, or until slightly charred, turning occasionally.

2 Add the pine nuts to the tin. Return to the oven and bake for 10 minutes, or until the pine nuts are toasted. Remove from the oven and allow the vegetables to cool completely.

3 Bring a large pan of lightly salted water to a rolling boil. Add the macaroni and cook according to the packet instructions, or until 'al dente'. Drain and refresh under cold running water then drain thoroughly and place in a large salad bowl.

4 Cut the turkey into bite-sized pieces and add to the macaroni. Add the artichokes and tomatoes with the cooled vegetables and pan juices to the pan. Blend together the coriander, garlic, remaining oil, vinegar and seasoning. Pour over the salad, toss lightly and serve.

## INGREDIENTS
### Serves 4

6 tbsp olive oil

3 medium courgettes, trimmed and sliced

2 yellow peppers, deseeded and sliced

125 g/4 oz pine nuts

275 g/10 oz macaroni

350 g/12 oz cooked turkey

280 g jar or can chargrilled artichokes, drained and sliced

225 g/8 oz baby plum tomatoes, quartered

4 tbsp freshly chopped coriander

1 garlic clove, peeled and chopped

3 tbsp balsamic vinegar

salt and freshly ground black pepper

## Helpful Hint

Other vegetables would be equally delicious. Try baby aubergines, trimmed and quartered lengthwise, or scrubbed new potatoes. If you cannot find chargrilled artichokes, use ordinary ones: drain and pat dry, then add to 1 tablespoon of hot olive oil in a frying pan and cook for 2–3 minutes, or until lightly charred.

# Spicy Chicken & Pasta Salad

**1** Bring a large pan of lightly salted water to a rolling boil. Add the pasta shells and cook according to the packet instructions, or until 'al dente'. Drain and refresh under cold running water then drain thoroughly and place in a large serving bowl.

**2** Meanwhile, melt the butter in a heavy-based pan, add the onion and cook for 5 minutes, or until softened. Add the curry paste and cook, stirring, for 2 minutes. Stir in the apricots and tomato paste, then cook for 1 minute. Remove from the heat and allow to cool.

**3** Blend the mango chutney and mayonnaise together in a small bowl. Drain the pineapple slices, adding 2 tablespoons of the pineapple juice to the mayonnaise mixture; reserve the pineapple slices. Season the mayonnaise to taste with salt and pepper.

**4** Cut the pineapple slices into chunks and stir into the pasta together with the mayonnaise mixture, curry paste and cooked chicken pieces. Toss lightly together to coat the pasta. Sprinkle with the almond slivers, garnish with coriander sprigs and serve.

## INGREDIENTS
*Serves 6*

450 g/1 lb pasta shells
25 g/1 oz butter
1 onion, peeled and chopped
2 tbsp mild curry paste
125 g/4 oz ready-to-eat dried
   apricots, chopped
2 tbsp tomato paste
3 tbsp mango chutney
300 ml/½ pint mayonnaise
425 g can pineapple slices in
   fruit juice
salt and freshly ground black
   pepper
450 g/1 lb skinned and boned
   cooked chicken, cut into bite-
   sized pieces
25 g/1 oz flaked toasted almond
   slivers
coriander sprigs, to garnish

## Helpful Hint

If you cannot buy almonds slivers, you can prepare your own. Place whole or half blanched almonds in a small bowl and pour over plenty of boiling water. Leave to soak for 20 minutes, then drain the almonds and cut into slivers using a sharp knife. Spread on a foil-lined grill pan and toast under a low grill for 1–2 minutes to make them dry and crunchy again.

# Chicken Gorgonzola & Mushroom Macaroni

1 Bring a large pan of lightly salted water to a rolling boil. Add the macaroni and cook according to the packet instructions, or until 'al dente'.

2 Meanwhile, melt the butter in a large frying pan, add the chestnut and button mushrooms and cook for 5 minutes, or until golden, stirring occasionally. Add the chicken to the pan and cook for 4 minutes, or until heated through thoroughly and slightly golden, stirring occasionally.

3 Blend the cornflour with a little of the milk in a jug to form a smooth paste, then gradually blend in the remaining milk and pour into the frying pan. Bring to the boil slowly, stirring constantly. Add cheese and cook for 1 minute, stirring frequently until melted.

4 Stir the sage and chives into the frying pan. Season to taste with salt and pepper then heat through. Drain the macaroni thoroughly and return to the pan. Pour the chicken and mushroom sauce over the macaroni and toss lightly to coat. Tip into a warmed serving dish, and serve immediately with extra Gorgonzola cheese.

## INGREDIENTS
*Serves 4*

*450 g/1 lb macaroni*
*75 g/3 oz butter*
*225 g/8 oz chestnut mushrooms, wiped and sliced*
*225 g/8 oz baby button mushrooms, wiped and halved*
*350 g/12 oz cooked chicken, skinned and chopped*
*2 tsp cornflour*
*300 ml/½ pint semi-skimmed milk*
*50 g/2 oz Gorgonzola cheese, chopped, plus extra to serve*
*2 tbsp freshly chopped sage*
*1 tbsp freshly chopped chives, plus extra chive leaves to garnish*
*salt and freshly ground black pepper*

## Food Fact

First mentioned in AD 879, Gorgonzola is the oldest named cheese in the world. It was named after the Italian town where cattle rested on their annual return from their summer pastures to their winter stalls. The original *piccante* is firm and heavily blue-veined with a strong flavour, while *dolce*, often simply labelled extra creamy, has a milder taste and a softer texture.

# Spaghetti with Turkey & Bacon Sauce

1 Bring a large pan of lightly salted water to a rolling boil. Add the spaghetti and cook according to the packet instructions, or until 'al dente'.

2 Meanwhile, melt the butter in a large frying pan. Using a sharp knife, cut the streaky bacon into small dice. Add the bacon to the pan with the turkey strips and cook for 8 minutes, or until browned, stirring occasionally to prevent sticking. Add the onion and garlic and cook for 5 minutes, or until softened, stirring occasionally.

3 Place the eggs and cream in a bowl and season to taste with salt and pepper. Beat together then pour into the frying pan and cook, stirring, for 2 minutes or until the mixture begins to thicken but does not scramble.

4 Drain the spaghetti thoroughly and return to the pan. Pour over the sauce, add the grated Parmesan cheese and toss lightly. Heat through for 2 minutes, or until piping hot. Tip into a warmed serving dish and sprinkle with freshly chopped coriander. Serve immediately.

## INGREDIENTS
### Serves 4

450 g / 1 lb spaghetti
25 g / 1 oz butter
225 g / 8 oz smoked streaky bacon, rind removed
350 g / 12 oz fresh turkey strips
1 onion, peeled and chopped
1 garlic clove, peeled and chopped
3 medium eggs, beaten
300 ml / ½ pint double cream
salt and freshly ground black pepper
50 g / 2 oz freshly grated Parmesan cheese
2–3 tbsp freshly chopped coriander, to garnish

## Helpful Hint

It is a good idea to remove the pan from the heat before adding the beaten eggs to the pan, as there should be enough residual heat in the sauce to cook them. If the sauce does not start to thicken after 2 minutes, return to a very low heat and continue cooking gently until it does.

# Cheesy Baked Chicken Macaroni

1 Preheat the grill just before cooking. Heat the oil in large frying pan and cook the chicken for 8 minutes, or until browned, stirring occasionally. Drain on absorbent kitchen paper and reserve. Add the pancetta slices to the pan and fry on both sides until crispy. Remove from the pan and reserve.

2 Add the onion and garlic to the frying pan and cook for 5 minutes, or until softened. Stir in the tomato sauce, chopped tomatoes and basil and season to taste with salt and pepper. Bring to the boil, lower the heat and simmer the sauce for 5 minutes.

3 Meanwhile, bring a large pan of lightly salted water to a rolling boil. Add the macaroni and cook according to the packet instructions, or until 'al dente'.

4 Drain the macaroni thoroughly, return to the pan and stir in the sauce, chicken and mozzarella cheese. Spoon into a shallow ovenproof dish.

5 Sprinkle the pancetta over the macaroni. Sprinkle over the Gruyère and Parmesan cheeses. Place under the preheated grill and cook for 5–10 minutes, or until golden-brown; turn the dish occasionally. Garnish and serve immediately.

## INGREDIENTS
*Serves 4*

1 tbsp olive oil
350 g/12 oz boneless and skinless chicken breasts, diced
75 g/3 oz pancetta, diced
1 onion, peeled and chopped
1 garlic clove, peeled and chopped
350 g packet fresh tomato sauce
400 g can chopped tomatoes
2 tbsp freshly chopped basil, plus leaves to garnish
salt and freshly ground black pepper
350 g/12 oz macaroni
150 g/5oz mozzarella cheese, drained and chopped
50 g/2 oz Gruyère cheese, grated
50 g/2 oz freshly grated Parmesan cheese

## Tasty Tip

This dish can be made with any pasta shape or flavour; try green spinach pasta for a change. Check the contents of the packet of fresh tomato sauce carefully; it may already contain herbs and spices, so you may need to cut out or reduce the garlic and fresh basil accordingly.

## Food Fact

Pancetta (cured dried belly of pork) imparts a wonderful flavour to a dish; it is available from Italian delicatessens.

# Spicy Mexican Chicken

**1** Heat the oil in a large frying pan, add the chicken mince and cook for 5 minutes, stirring frequently with a wooden spoon to break up any lumps. Add the onion, garlic and pepper and cook for 3 minutes, stirring occasionally. Stir in the chilli powder and cook for a further 2 minutes.

**2** Stir in the tomato paste, pour in the chicken stock and season to taste with salt and pepper. Bring to the boil, reduce the heat, and simmer, covered, for 20 minutes.

**3** Add the kidney and chilli beans and cook, stirring occasionally, for 10 minutes, or until the chicken is tender.

**4** Meanwhile, bring a large pan of lightly salted water to a rolling boil. Add the spaghetti and cook according to the packet instructions, or until 'al dente'.

**5** Drain the spaghetti thoroughly, arrange on warmed plates and spoon over the chicken and bean mixture. Serve with the grated cheese, guacamole and salsa.

## INGREDIENTS
*Serves 4*

*2 tbsp olive oil*
*450 g/1 lb chicken mince*
*1 red onion, peeled and chopped*
*2 garlic cloves, peeled and chopped*
*1 red pepper, deseeded and*
  *chopped*
*1–2 tsp hot chilli powder*
*2 tbsp tomato paste*
*225 ml/8 fl oz chicken stock*
*salt and freshly ground black*
  *pepper*
*420 g can red kidney beans,*
  *drained*
*420 g can chilli beans, drained*
*350 g/12 oz spaghetti*

*TO SERVE:*
*Monterey Jack or Cheddar cheese,*
  *grated*
*guacamole*
*hot chilli salsa*

## Helpful Hint

A variety of chilli powders are available. The most usual is the red powder made from dried red chillies, which may be mild or hot. A darker powder, which contains a mixture of ground chilli and herbs, is specifically for use in Mexican and southwest American dishes.

# Pesto Chicken Tagliatelle

**1** Heat the oil in a large frying pan, add the chicken and cook for 8 minutes, or until golden-brown, stirring occasionally. Using a slotted spoon, remove the chicken from the pan, drain on absorbent kitchen paper and reserve.

**2** Melt the butter in the pan. Add the leeks and cook for 3–5 minutes, or until slightly softened, stirring occasionally. Add the oyster and chestnut mushrooms and cook for 5 minutes, or until browned, stirring occasionally.

**3** Bring a large pan of lightly salted water to the boil, add the tagliatelle, return to the boil and cook for 4 minutes, or until 'al dente'.

**4** Add the chicken, pesto and crème fraîche to the mushroom mixture. Stir, then heat through thoroughly. Stir in the grated Parmesan cheese and season to taste with salt and pepper.

**5** Drain the tagliatelle thoroughly and pile on to warmed plates. Spoon over the sauce and serve immediately.

## INGREDIENTS
### Serves 4

2 tbsp olive oil

350 g/12 oz boneless and skinless chicken breasts, cut into chunks

75 g/3 oz butter

2 medium leeks, trimmed and sliced thinly

125 g/4 oz oyster mushrooms, trimmed and halved

200 g/7 oz small open chestnut mushrooms, wiped and halved

450 g/1lb fresh tagliatelle

4–6 tbsp red pesto

200 ml/7 fl oz crème fraîche

50 g/2 oz freshly grated Parmesan cheese

salt and freshly ground black pepper

## Food Fact

Classic pesto is green because it is made from basil. Red pesto is made from a purée of sun-dried tomatoes. Both types of pesto make great store-cupboard standbys as they can be simply tossed with cooked pasta for the speediest of meals. They are even more wonderful livened up with a little crème fraîche, as here, or mascarpone cheese.

# Chicken & Prawn-stacked Ravioli

1 Heat the olive oil in a large frying pan, add the onion and garlic and cook for 5 minutes, or until softened, stirring occasionally. Add the chicken pieces and fry for 4 minutes, or until heated through, turning occasionally.

2 Stir in the chopped tomato, wine and cream and bring to the boil. Lower the heat and simmer for about 5 minutes, or until reduced and thickened. Stir in the prawns and tarragon and season to taste with salt and pepper. Heat the sauce through gently.

3 Meanwhile, bring a large pan of lightly salted water to the boil and add 2 lasagne sheets. Return to the boil and cook for 2 minutes, stirring gently to avoid sticking. Remove from the pan using a slotted spoon and keep warm. Repeat with the remaining sheets.

4 Cut each sheet of lasagne in half. Place two pieces on each of the warmed plates and divide half of the chicken mixture among them. Top each serving with a second sheet of lasagne and divide the remainder of the chicken mixture among them. Top with a final layer of lasagne. Garnish with tarragon sprigs and serve immediately.

## INGREDIENTS
### Serves 4

1 tbsp olive oil
1 onion, peeled and chopped
1 garlic clove, peeled and chopped
450 g/1 lb boned and skinned cooked chicken, cut into large pieces
1 beefsteak tomato, deseeded and chopped
150 ml/¼ pint dry white wine
150 ml/¼ pint double cream
250 g/9 oz peeled cooked prawns, thawed if frozen
2 tbsp freshly chopped tarragon, plus sprigs to garnish
salt and freshly ground black pepper
8 sheets fresh lasagne

## Helpful Hint

Always check the packet instructions when cooking lasagne; some brands may need longer cooking than others. It should be cooked until 'al dente' – tender, but firm to the bite. Dried lasagne – either plain or verde – may be used instead of fresh if preferred, but it will take longer to cook.

# Penne with Pan-fried Chicken & Capers

**1** Trim the chicken and cut into bite-sized pieces. Season the flour with salt and pepper then toss the chicken in the seasoned flour and reserve.

**2** Bring a large saucepan of lightly salted water to a rolling boil. Add the penne and cook according to the packet instructions, or until 'al dente'.

**3** Meanwhile, heat the olive oil in a large frying pan. Add the chicken to the pan and cook for 8 minutes, or until golden on all sides, stirring frequently. Transfer the chicken to a plate and reserve.

**4** Add the onion and garlic to the oil remaining in the frying pan and cook for 5 minutes, or until softened, stirring frequently.

**5** Return the chicken to the frying pan. Stir in the pesto and mascarpone cheese and heat through, stirring gently, until smooth. Stir in the wholegrain mustard, lemon juice, basil and capers. Season to taste, then continue to heat through until piping hot.

**6** Drain the penne thoroughly and return to the saucepan. Pour over the sauce and toss well to coat. Arrange the pasta on individual warmed plates. Scatter with the cheese and serve immediately.

## Food Fact

Pecorino Romano is a cooked, pressed cheese made in dairies in and around Rome. It is similar to Parmesan (which may be used instead, if preferred) with a dense texture, pale yellow colour and almost smoky aroma. Its flavour is very salty, so take care when seasoning the pasta and chicken when cooking.

### INGREDIENTS
*Serves 4*

*4 boneless and skinless chicken breasts*
*25 g/1 oz plain flour*
*salt and freshly ground black pepper*
*350 g/12 oz penne*
*2 tbsp olive oil*
*25 g/1 oz butter*
*1 red onion, peeled and sliced*
*1 garlic clove, peeled and chopped*
*4–6 tbsp pesto*
*250 g carton mascarpone cheese*
*1 tsp wholegrain mustard*
*1 tbsp lemon juice*
*2 tbsp freshly chopped basil*
*3 tbsp capers in brine, rinsed and drained*
*freshly shaved Pecorino Romano cheese*

# Spaghetti with Pesto

1 To make the pesto, place the Parmesan cheese in a food processor with the basil leaves, pine nuts and garlic and process until well blended.

2 With the motor running, gradually pour in the extra virgin olive oil, until a thick sauce forms. Add a little more oil if the sauce seems too thick. Season to taste with salt and pepper. Transfer to a bowl, cover and store in the refrigerator until required.

3 Bring a large pan of lightly salted water to a rolling boil. Add the spaghetti and cook according to the packet instructions, or until 'al dente'.

4 Drain the spaghetti thoroughly and return to the pan. Stir in the pesto and toss lightly. Heat through gently, then tip the pasta into a warmed serving dish or spoon on to individual plates. Garnish with basil leaves and serve immediately with extra Parmesan cheese.

## INGREDIENTS
### Serves 4

200 g/7 oz freshly grated Parmesan cheese, plus extra to serve

25 g/1 oz fresh basil leaves, plus extra to garnish

6 tbsp pine nuts

3 large garlic cloves, peeled

200 ml/7 fl oz extra virgin olive oil, plus more if necessary

salt and freshly ground pepper

400 g/14 oz spaghetti

## Helpful Hint

You can still make pesto if you do not have a food processor. Tear the basil leaves and place them in a mortar with the garlic, pine nuts and a tablespoonful of the oil. Pound to a paste using a pestle, gradually working in the rest of the oil. Transfer to a bowl and stir in the cheese. Season to taste with salt and pepper. Pesto will keep for 2–3 days if stored in the refrigerator.

# Pasta Shells with Broccoli & Capers

1 Bring a large pan of lightly salted water to a rolling boil. Add the orecchiette, return to the boil and cook for 2 minutes. Add the broccoli to the pan. Return to the boil and continue cooking for 8–10 minutes, or until the conchiglie is 'al dente'.

2 Meanwhile, heat the olive oil in a large frying pan, add the onion and cook for 5 minutes, or until softened, stirring frequently. Stir in the capers and chilli flakes, if using, and cook for a further 2 minutes.

3 Drain the pasta and broccoli and add to the frying pan. Toss the ingredients to mix thoroughly. Sprinkle over the cheeses, then stir until the cheeses have just melted. Season to taste with salt and pepper, then tip into a warmed serving dish. Garnish with chopped parsley and serve immediately with extra Parmesan cheese.

## INGREDIENTS
### Serves 4

*400 g/14 oz conchiglie (shells)*
*450 g/1 lb broccoli florets, cut into small pieces*
*5 tbsp olive oil*
*1 large onion, peeled and finely chopped*
*4 tbsp capers in brine, rinsed and drained*
*½ tsp dried chilli flakes (optional)*
*75 g/3 oz freshly grated Parmesan cheese, plus extra to serve*
*25 g/1 oz pecorino cheese, grated*
*salt and freshly ground black pepper*
*2 tbsp freshly chopped flat-leaf parsley, to garnish*

## Helpful Hint

Chilli flakes are made from dried, crushed chillies and add a pungent hot spiciness to this dish. There are lots of other chilli products that you could use instead. For instance, substitute a tablespoonful of chilli oil for one of the tablespoons of olive oil or add a dash of Tabasco sauce at the end of cooking.

# Venetian Herb Orzo

1 Rinse the spinach leaves in several changes of cold water and reserve. Finely chop the rocket leaves with the parsley and mint. Thinly slice the green of the spring onions.

2 Bring a large saucepan of water to the boil, add the spinach leaves, herbs and spring onions and cook for about 10 seconds. Remove and rinse under cold running water. Drain well and, using your hands, squeeze out all the excess moisture.

3 Place the spinach, herbs and spring onions in a food processor. Blend for 1 minute then, with the motor running, gradually pour in the olive oil until the sauce is well blended.

4 Meanwhile, bring a large pan of lightly salted water to a rolling boil. Add the pasta and cook according to the packet instructions, or until 'al dente'. Drain thoroughly and place in a large warmed bowl.

5 Add the spinach sauce to the orzo and stir lightly until the orzo is well coated. Stir in an extra tablespoon of olive oil if the mixture seems too thick. Season well with salt and pepper. Serve immediately on warmed plates or allow to cool to room temperature.

## INGREDIENTS
### Serves 4-6

200 g/7 oz baby spinach leaves
150 g/5 oz rocket leaves
50 g/2 oz flat-leaf parsley
6 spring onions, trimmed
few leaves of fresh mint
3 tbsp extra virgin olive oil, plus
   more if required
450 g/11 oz orzo
salt and freshly ground black
   pepper

## Food Fact

Rocket was first introduced to Britain in the late sixteenth century, but went out of fashion during Victorian times. It adds a peppery flavour to many dishes. The tender tiny leaves have the most delicate flavour and as they grow in size the flavour becomes more pronounced.

# Cheesy Pasta with Tomatoes & Cream

**1** Place the ricotta cheese in a bowl and beat until smooth, then add the remaining cheeses with the eggs, herbs and seasoning to taste. Beat well until creamy and smooth.

**2** Cut the prepared pasta dough into quarters. Working with one-quarter at a time, and covering the remaining quarters with a clean, damp tea towel, roll out the pasta very thinly. Using a 10 cm/4 inch pastry cutter or small saucer, cut out as many rounds as possible.

**3** Place a small tablespoonful of the filling mixture slightly below the centre of each round. Lightly moisten the edge of the round with water and fold in half to form a filled half-moon shape. Using a dinner fork, press the edges together firmly.

**4** Transfer to a lightly floured baking sheet and continue filling the remaining pasta. Leave to dry for 15 minutes.

**5** Heat the oil in a large saucepan, add the onions and cook for 3–4 minutes, or until beginning to soften. Add the garlic and cook for 1–2 minutes, then add the tomatoes, vermouth and cream and bring to the boil. Simmer for 10–15 minutes, or until thickened and reduced.

**6** Bring a large saucepan of salted water to the boil. Add the filled pasta and return to the boil. Cook, stirring frequently to prevent sticking, for 5 minutes, or until 'al dente'. Drain and return to the pan. Pour over the tomato and cream sauce, garnish with basil leaves and serve immediately.

## INGREDIENTS
### Serves 4

225 g/8 oz fresh ricotta cheese

225 g/8 oz smoked mozzarella, grated, (use normal if smoked is unavailable)

5 g/4 oz freshly grated pecorino or Parmesan cheese

2 medium eggs, lightly beated

2–3 tbsp finely chopped mint, basil or parsley

salt and freshly ground black pepper

### FOR THE SAUCE:

2 tbsp olive oil

1 small onion, peeled and finely chopped

2 garlic cloves, peeled and finely chopped

450g/1 lb ripe plum tomatoes, peeled, deseeded and finely chopped

50 ml/2 fl oz white vermouth

225 ml/8 fl oz double cream

fresh basil leaves, to garnish

# Pastini-stuffed Peppers

1 Preheat the oven to 190°C/ 375°F/Gas Mark 5, 10 minutes before cooking. Bring a pan of water to the boil. Trim the bottom of each pepper so it sits straight. Blanch the peppers for 2–3 minutes, then drain on absorbent kitchen paper.

2 Return the water to the boil, add ½ teaspoon of salt and the pastini and cook for 3–4 minutes, or until 'al dente'. Drain thoroughly, reserving the water. Rinse under cold running water, drain again and reserve.

3 Heat 2 tablespoons of the olive oil in a large frying pan, add the onion and cook for 3–4 minutes. Add the garlic and cook for 1 minute. Stir in the tomatoes and wine and cook for 5 minutes, stirring frequently. Add the olives, herbs, mozzarella cheese and half the Parmesan cheese. Season to taste with salt and pepper. Remove from the heat and stir in the pastini.

4 Dry the insides of the peppers with absorbent kitchen paper, then season lightly. Arrange the peppers in a lightly oiled shallow baking dish and fill with the pastini mixture. Sprinkle with the remaining Parmesan cheese and drizzle over the remaining oil. Pour in boiling water to come 1 cm/½ inch up the sides of the dish. Cook in the preheated oven for 25 minutes, or until cooked. Serve immediately with freshly made tomato sauce.

## INGREDIENTS
### Serves 6

6 red, yellow or orange peppers, tops cut off and deseeded
salt and freshly ground black pepper
175 g/6 oz pastini
4 tbsp olive oil
1 onion, peeled and finely chopped
2 garlic cloves, peeled and finely chopped
3 ripe plum tomatoes, skinned, deseeded and chopped
50 ml/2 fl oz dry white wine
8 pitted black olives, chopped
4 tbsp freshly chopped mixed herbs, such as parsley, basil, oregano or marjoram
125 g/4 oz mozzarella cheese, diced
4 tbsp grated Parmesan cheese
fresh tomato sauce, preferably home-made, to serve

## Tasty Tip

For a rich tomato sauce, roughly chop 900 g/2 lb ripe tomatoes, then place in a saucepan with 1 crushed garlic clove, 1 tablespoon olive oil and 2 tablespoons Worcestershire sauce. Cook until soft, sieve or purèe and serve with the peppers.

# Fusilli with Courgettes & Sun-dried Tomatoes

1 Heat 2 tablespoons of the olive oil in a large frying pan, add the onion and cook for 5–7 minutes, or until softened. Add the chopped garlic and courgette slices and cook for a further 5 minutes, stirring occasionally.

2 Stir the chopped tomatoes and the sun-dried tomatoes into the frying pan and season to taste with salt and pepper. Cook until the courgettes are just tender and the sauce is slightly thickened.

3 Bring a large pan of lightly salted water to a rolling boil. Add the fusilli and cook according to the packet instructions, or until 'al dente'.

4 Drain the fusilli thoroughly and return to the pan. Add the butter and remaining oil and toss to coat. Stir the chopped basil or parsley into the courgette mixture and pour over the fusilli. Toss and tip into a warmed serving dish. Serve with grated Parmesan or pecorino cheese.

## INGREDIENTS
*Serves 6*

*5 tbsp olive oil*
*1 large onion, peeled and thinly sliced*
*2 garlic cloves, peeled and finely chopped*
*700 g / 1½ lb courgettes, trimmed and sliced*
*400 g can chopped plum tomatoes*
*12 sun-dried tomatoes, cut into thin strips*
*salt and freshly ground black pepper*
*450 g / 1 lb fusilli*
*25 g / 1 oz butter, diced*
*2 tbsp freshly chopped basil or flat-leaf parsley*
*grated Parmesan or pecorino cheese, for serving*

## Food Fact

Sun-dried tomatoes come in jars with olive oil or simply dried in packets, in which case they will need re-hydrating. The latter are better for this recipe as they will soak up the juices from the chopped tomatoes and courgettes and help to thicken the sauce.

# Linguine with Walnut Pesto

1 Bring a saucepan of water to the boil. Add the walnut halves and simmer for about 1 minute. Drain and turn on to a clean tea towel. Using the towel, rub the nuts gently to loosen the skins, turn into a coarse sieve or colander and shake to separate the skins. Discard the skins and coarsely chop the nuts.

2 With the the food processor motor running, drop in the garlic cloves and chop finely. Remove the lid, then add the walnuts, breadcrumbs, olive and walnut oils and the parsley. Blend to a paste with a crumbly texture.

3 Scrape the nut mixture into a bowl, add the softened butter and, using a wooden spoon, cream them together.

Gradually beat in the cream and the Parmesan cheese. Season the walnut pesto to taste with salt and pepper.

4 Bring a large pan of lightly salted water to a rolling boil. Add the linguine and cook according to the packet instructions, or until 'al dente'.

5 Drain the linguine thoroughly, reserving 1–2 tablespoons of the cooking water. Return the linguine and reserved water to the pan. Add the walnut pesto, 1 tablespoon at a time, tossing and stirring until well coated. Tip into a warmed serving dish or spoon on to individual plates. Serve immediately with the extra grated Parmesan cheese.

## Helpful Hint

It is important to use dried breadcrumbs for this recipe. Avoid the bright orange variety, which are unsuitable. Spread about 50 g/2 oz fresh breadcrumbs (they will weigh less when dried) on a baking sheet and bake in a very low oven for about 20–25 minutes, stirring occasionally, until dry but not coloured.

## INGREDIENTS
### Serves 4

125 g/4 oz walnut halves
1–2 garlic cloves, peeled and coarsely chopped
40 g/1 ½ oz dried breadcrumbs
3 tbsp extra virgin olive oil
1 tbsp walnut oil
3–4 tbsp freshly chopped parsley
50 g/2 oz butter, softened
2 tbsp double cream
25 g/1 oz Parmesan cheese, grated, plus extra to serve
salt and freshly ground black pepper
450 g/1 lb linguine

# Four-cheese Tagliatelle

**1** Place the whipping cream with the garlic cloves in a medium pan and heat gently until small bubbles begin to form around the edge of the pan. Using a slotted spoon, remove and discard the garlic cloves.

**2** Add all the cheeses to the pan and stir until melted. Season with a little salt and a lot of black pepper. Keep the sauce warm over a low heat, but do not allow to boil.

**3** Meanwhile, bring a large pan of lightly salted water to the boil. Add the taglietelle, return to the boil and cook for 2–3 minutes, or until 'al dente'.

**4** Drain the pasta thoroughly and return to the pan. Pour the sauce over the pasta, add the chives then toss lightly until well coated. Tip into a warmed serving dish or spoon on to individual plates. Garnish with a few basil leaves and serve immediately with extra Parmesan cheese.

## INGREDIENTS
*Serves 4*

*300 ml/½ pint whipping cream*
*4 garlic cloves, peeled and lightly bruised*
*75 g/3 oz fontina cheese, diced*
*75 g/3 oz Gruyère cheese, grated*
*75 g/3 oz mozzarella cheese, preferably, diced*
*50 g/2 oz Parmesan cheese, grated, plus extra to serve*
*salt and freshly ground black pepper*
*275 g/10 oz fresh green tagliatelle*
*1–2 tbsp freshly snipped chives*
*fresh basil leaves, to garnish*

## Helpful Hint

Fresh pasta takes much less time to cook than dried pasta and 2–3 minutes is usually long enough for it to be 'al dente', but check the packet for cooking instructions. Tagliatelle comes from Bologna, where it is usually served with a meat sauce. Green tagliatelle is generally flavoured with spinach, but it is also available flavoured with fresh herbs, which would go particularly well with the rich cheese sauce in this recipe.

# Spaghetti alla Puttanesca

**1** Heat the olive oil in a large frying pan, add the anchovies and cook, stirring with a wooden spoon and crushing the anchovies, until they disintegrate. Add the garlic and dried chillies and cook for 1 minute, stirring frequently.

**2** Add the tomatoes, olives, capers, oregano and tomato paste and cook, stirring occasionally, for 15 minutes, or until the liquid has evaporated and the sauce is thickened. Season the tomato sauce to taste with salt and pepper.

**3** Meanwhile, bring a large pan of lightly salted water to a rolling boil. Add the spaghetti and cook according to the packet instructions, or until 'al dente'.

**4** Drain the spaghetti thoroughly, reserving 1–2 tablespoons of the the cooking water. Return the spaghetti with the reserved water to the pan. Pour the tomato sauce over the spaghetti, add the chopped parsley and toss to coat. Tip into a warmed serving dish or spoon on to individual plates and serve immediately.

## INGREDIENTS
*Serves 4*

4 tbsp olive oil

50 g/2 oz anchovy fillets in olive oil, drained and coarsely chopped

2 garlic cloves, peeled and finely chopped

½ tsp crushed dried chillies

400 g can chopped plum tomatoes

125 g/4 oz pitted black olives, cut in half

2 tbsp capers, rinsed and drained

1 tsp freshly chopped oregano

1 tbsp tomato paste

salt and freshly ground black pepper

400 g/14 oz spaghetti

2 tbsp freshly chopped parsley

## Helpful Hint

Anchovies are mature sardines. They are heavily salted after filleting to preserve them, so should only be used in small quantities. For a less salty dish, drain them and soak in a little milk for about 20 minutes before using. You can, of course, omit the anchovies to make a vegetarian version of this recipe.

# Tagliatelle Primavera

1 Bring a medium saucepan of salted water to the boil. Add the asparagus and blanch for 1–2 minutes, or until just beginning to soften. Using a slotted spoon, transfer to a colander and rinse under cold running water. Repeat with the carrots and courgettes. Add the mangetout, return to the boil, drain, rinse immediately and drain again. Reserve the blanched vegetables.

2 Heat the butter in a large frying pan, add the onion and red pepper and cook for 5 minutes, or until they begin to soften and colour. Pour in the dry vermouth; it will bubble and steam and evaporate almost immediately. Stir in the cream and simmer over a medium-low heat until reduced by about half. Add the blanched vegetables with the leeks, peas and seasoning and heat through for 2 minutes.

3 Meanwhile, bring a large saucepan of lightly salted water to the boil, add the tagliatelle and return to the boil. Cook for 2-3 minutes, or until 'al dente'. Drain thoroughly and return to the pan.

4 Stir the chopped parsley into the cream and vegetable sauce then pour over the pasta and toss to coat. Sprinkle with the grated Parmesan cheese and toss lightly. Tip into a warmed serving bowl or spoon on to individual plates and serve immediately.

## INGREDIENTS
### Serves 4

125 g/4 oz asparagus, lightly peeled and cut into 6.5 cm/2½ inch lengths

125 g/4 oz carrots, peeled and cut into julienne strips

125 g/4 oz courgettes, trimmed and cut into julienne strips

50 g/2 oz small mangetout

50 g/2 oz butter

1 small onion, peeled and finely chopped

1 small red pepper, deseeded and finely chopped

50 ml/2 fl oz dry vermouth

225 ml/8 fl oz double cream

1 small leek, trimmed and cut into julienne strips

75 g/3 oz fresh green peas (or frozen, thawed)

salt and freshly ground black pepper

400 g/14 oz fresh tagliatelle

2 tbsp freshly chopped flat-leaf parsley

25 g/1 oz Parmesan cheese, grated

## Helpful Hint

If using baby asparagus spears – readily available in most major supermarkets – there is no need to peel the stems. This is only necessary on the long spears which can have a woody stalk as the season progresses.

# Aubergine & Ravioli Parmigiana

1 Preheat the oven to 180°C/ 350°F/Gas Mark 4, about 15 minutes before cooking. Heat 2 tablespoons of the olive oil in a large, heavy-based pan, add the onion and cook for 6–7 minutes, or until softened. Add the garlic, cook for 1 minute then stir in the tomatoes, sugar, bay leaf, dried oregano and basil, then bring to the boil, stirring frequently. Simmer for 30–35 minutes, or until thickened and reduced, stirring occasionally. Stir in the fresh basil and season to taste with salt and pepper. Remove the tomato sauce from the heat and reserve.

2 Heat the remaining olive oil in a large, heavy-based frying pan over a high heat. Dip the aubergine slices in the egg mixture then in the breadcrumbs.

Cook in batches until golden on both sides. Drain on absorbent kitchen paper. Add more oil between batches if necessary.

3 Spoon a little tomato sauce into the base of a lightly oiled large baking dish. Cover with a layer of aubergine slices, a sprinkling of Parmesan cheese, a layer of mozzarella cheese, then more sauce. Repeat the layers then cover the sauce with a layer of cooked ravioli. Continue to layer in this way, ending with a layer of mozzarella cheese. Sprinkle the top with Parmesan cheese.

4 Drizzle with a little extra olive oil if liked, then bake in the preheated oven for 30 minutes, or until golden-brown and bubbling. Serve immediately.

## Helpful Hint

Aubergines absorb a huge amount of oil during cooking, so use a good non-stick frying pan and gradually add oil as required. You can use baby aubergines for this recipe if you prefer. Trim off the stalk ends, then cut them lengthwise into 1 cm/½ inch strips.

*INGREDIENTS*
*Serves 6*

4 tbsp olive oil

1 large onion, peeled and finely
   chopped

2–3 garlic cloves, peeled and
   crushed

2 x 400 g cans chopped tomatoes

2 tsp brown sugar

1 dried bay leaf

1 tsp dried oregano

1 tsp dried basil

2 tbsp freshly shredded basil

salt and freshly ground black
   pepper

2–3 medium aubergines, sliced
   crosswwise 1 cm/½ inch thick

2 medium eggs, beaten with
   1 tbsp water

125 g/4 oz dried breadcrumbs

75 g/3 oz freshly grated
   Parmesan cheese

400 g/14 oz mozzarella cheese,
   thinly sliced

250 g/9 oz cheese-filled ravioli,
   cooked and drained

# Courgette Lasagne

1 Preheat the oven to 200°C/ 400°F/Gas Mark 6, 15 minutes before cooking. Heat the oil in a large frying pan, add the onion and cook for 3–5 minutes. Add the mushrooms, cook for 2 minutes then add the courgettes and cook for a further 3–4 minutes, or until tender. Stir in the garlic, thyme and basil or parsley and season to taste with salt and pepper. Remove from the heat and reserve.

2 Spoon one-third of the white sauce on to the base of a lightly oiled large baking dish. Arrange a layer of lasagne over the sauce. Spread half the courgette mixture over the pasta, then sprinkle with some of the mozzarella and some of the Parmesan cheese. Repeat with more white sauce and another layer of lasagne, then cover with half the drained tomatoes.

3 Cover the tomatoes with lasagne, the remaining courgette mixture, and some mozzarella and Parmesan cheese. Repeat the layers ending with a layer of lasagne sheets, white sauce and the remaining Parmesan cheese. Bake in the preheated oven for 35 minutes, or until golden. Serve immediately.

## INGREDIENTS
### Serves 8

2 tbsp olive oil

1 medium onion, peeled and finely chopped

225 g/8 oz mushrooms, wiped and thinly sliced

3–4 courgettes, trimmed and thinly sliced

2 garlic cloves, peeled and finely chopped

½ tsp dried thyme

1–2 tbsp freshly chopped basil or flat-leaf parsley

salt and freshly ground black pepper

1 quantity prepared white sauce see page 98

350 g/12 oz lasagne sheets, cooked

225 g/8 oz mozzarella cheese, grated

50 g/2 oz Parmesan cheese, grated

400 g can chopped tomatoes, drained

## Helpful Hint

There is now a huge range of canned tomatoes available. Look out for canned cherry tomatoes, which have a much sweeter flavour, or those with added ingredients and flavourings. Tomatoes with chopped peppers, garlic or fresh herbs would all work well here and would add extra flavour.

# Baked Macaroni Cheese

1 Preheat the oven to 190°C/ 375°F/Gas Mark 5, 10 minutes before cooking. Bring a large pan of lightly salted water to a rolling boil. Add the macaroni and cook according to the packet instructions, or until 'al dente'. Drain thoroughly and reserve.

2 Meanwhile, melt 50 g/ 2 oz of the butter in a large, heavy-based saucepan, add the onion and cook, stirring frequently, for 5–7 minutes, or until softened. Sprinkle in the flour and cook, stirring constantly, for 2 minutes. Remove the pan from the heat, stir in the milk, return to the heat and cook, stirring, until a smooth sauce has formed.

3 Add the bay leaf and thyme to the sauce and season to taste with salt, pepper, cayenne pepper and freshly grated nutmeg. Simmer for about 15 minutes, stirring frequently, until thickened and smooth.

4 Remove the sauce from the heat. Add the cooked leeks, mustard and Cheddar cheese and stir until the cheese has melted. Stir in the macaroni then tip into a lightly oiled baking dish.

5 Sprinkle the breadcrumbs and Parmesan cheese over the macaroni. Dot with the remaining butter, then bake in the preheated oven for 1 hour, or until golden. Garnish with a basil sprig and serve immediately.

## INGREDIENTS
*Serves 8*

*450 g/1 lb macaroni*
*75 g/3 oz butter*
*1 onion, peeled and finely chopped*
*40 g/1½ oz plain flour*
*1 litre/1¾ pints milk*
*1–2 dried bay leaves*
*½ tsp dried thyme*
*salt and freshly ground black pepper*
*cayenne pepper*
*freshly grated nutmeg*
*2 small leeks, trimmed, finely chopped, cooked and drained*
*1 tbsp Dijon mustard*
*400 g/14 oz mature Cheddar cheese, grated*
*2 tbsp dried breadcrumbs*
*2 tbsp freshly grated Parmesan cheese*
*basil sprig, to garnish*

## Helpful Hint

Make sure that you only simmer the macaroni until just 'al dente' and drain straight away, as it will be further cooked in the oven where it needs to soak up the flavoursome sauce. For a more substantial dish, chopped, lean smoked bacon can be stirred into the macaroni before baking.

# Penne with Vodka & Caviar

1 Bring a large pan of lightly salted water to a rolling boil. Add the penne and cook according to the packet instructions, or until 'al dente'. Drain thoroughly and reserve.

2 Heat the butter in a large frying pan or wok, add the spring onions and stir-fry for 1 minute. Stir in the garlic and cook for a further 1 minute. Pour the vodka into the pan; it will bubble and steam. Cook until the vodka is reduced by about half, then add the double cream and return to the boil. Simmer gently for 2–3 minutes, or until the sauce has thickened slightly.

3 Stir in the tomatoes, then stir in all but 1 tablespoon of the caviar and season to taste with salt and pepper. Add the penne and toss lightly to coat. Cook for 1 minute, or until heated through. Divide the mixture among 4 warmed pasta bowls and garnish with the reserved caviar. Serve immediately.

## INGREDIENTS
### Serves 4

400 g/14 oz penne
25 g/1 oz butter
4–6 spring onions, trimmed and thinly sliced
1 garlic clove, peeled and finely chopped
125 ml/4 fl oz vodka
200 ml/7 fl oz double cream
1–2 ripe plum tomatoes, skinned, deseeded and chopped
75 g/3 oz caviar
salt and freshly ground black pepper

## Food Fact

Authentic sturgeon caviar is very expensive. Red caviar from salmon, or black or red lump-fish roe, can be substituted. Alternatively, 175 g/6 oz thinly sliced smoked salmon pieces, can also be substituted. Sturgeon caviar has a salty flavour, so always check the taste before adding salt. Smoked salmon and lump-fish roe have a much saltier taste, however, so no additional salt would be necessary.

# Rigatoni with Gorgonzola & Walnuts

1 Bring a large pan of lightly salted water to a rolling boil. Add the rigatoni and cook according to the packet instructions, or until 'al dente'. Drain the pasta thoroughly, reserve and keep warm.

2 Melt the butter in a large saucepan or wok over a medium heat. Add the Gorgonzola cheese and stir until just melted. Add the brandy if using and cook for 30 seconds, then pour in the cream and cook for 1–2 minutes, stirring until the sauce is smooth.

3 Stir in the walnut pieces, basil and half the Parmesan cheese, then add the rigatoni. Season to taste with salt and pepper. Return to the heat, stirring frequently, until heated through. Divide the pasta among 4 warmed pasta bowls, sprinkle with the remaining Parmesan cheese and serve immediately with cherry tomatoes and fresh green salad leaves.

## INGREDIENTS
### Serves 4

400 g/14 oz rigatoni
50 g/2 oz butter
125 g/4 oz crumbled Gorgonzola cheese
2 tbsp brandy, optional
200 ml/7 fl oz whipping or double cream
75 g/3 oz walnut pieces, lightly toasted and coarsely chopped
1 tbsp freshly chopped basil
50 g/2 oz freshly grated Parmesan cheese
salt and freshly ground black pepper

### TO SERVE:
cherry tomatoes
fresh green salad leaves

## Tasty Tip

This blue cheese sauce is also very good with pappardelle or lasagnette, both very wide egg pasta noodles. Either whipping or double cream may be used here; double cream is higher in fat, so will give a richer, creamier finish to the sauce. If preferred, you could use soured cream, but it must be heated gently as it can curdle at high temperatures.

# Pumpkin-filled Pasta with Butter & Sage

1 Mix together the ingredients for the filling in a bowl, seasoning to taste with freshly grated nutmeg, salt and pepper. If the mixture seems too wet, add a few more breadcrumbs to bind.

2 Cut the pasta dough into quarters. Work with one quarter at a time, covering the remaining quarters with a damp tea towel. Roll out a quarter very thinly into a strip 10 cm/ 4 inches wide. Drop spoonfuls of the filling along the strip 6.5 cm/2½ inches apart, in 2 rows about 5 cm/2 inches apart. Moisten the outside edges and the spaces between the filling with water.

3 Roll out another strip of pasta and lay it over the filled strip. Press down gently along both edges and between the filled sections. Using a fluted pastry wheel, cut along both long sides, down the centre and between the fillings to form cushions. Transfer the cushions to a lightly floured baking sheet. Continue making cushions and allow to dry for 30 minutes.

4 Bring a large saucepan of slightly salted water to the boil. Add the pasta cushions and return to the boil. Cook, stirring frequently, for 4–5 minutes, or until 'al dente'. Drain carefully.

5 Heat the butter in a pan, stir in the shredded sage leaves and cook for 30 seconds. Add the pasta cushions, stir gently then spoon into serving bowls. Sprinkle with the grated Parmesan cheese and serve immediately.

## INGREDIENTS
*Serves 6-8*

*1 quantity fresh pasta dough, see page 16*
*125 g/4 oz butter*
*2 tbsp freshly shredded sage leaves*
*50 g/2 oz freshly grated Parmesan cheese, to serve*

## FOR THE FILLING:
*250 g/9 oz freshly cooked pumpkin or sweet potato flesh, mashed and cooled*
*75–125 g/3–4 oz dried breadcrumbs*
*125 g/4 oz freshly grated Parmesan cheese*
*1 medium egg yolk*
*½ tsp soft brown sugar*
*2 tbsp freshly chopped parsley*
*freshly grated nutmeg*
*salt and freshly ground black pepper*

# Cold Sesame Noodles

1 Bring a large pan of lightly salted water to a rolling boil. Add the noodles or spaghetti and cook according to the packet instructions, or until 'al dente'. Drain, rinse and drain again, then toss in the sesame oil and reserve.

2 Heat the groundnut oil in a wok or large frying pan over a high heat. Add the green pepper, daikon and mangetout or green beans and stir-fry for 1 minute. Stir in the garlic and cook for 30 seconds.

3 Add the soy sauce to the pan with the vinegar, chilli sauce, sugar, peanut butter and 50 ml/2 fl oz of hot water. Simmer, stirring constantly, until the peanut butter is smooth, adding a little more water if necessary and adjusting the seasoning to taste.

4 Add the spring onions and the reserved noodles or spaghetti to the peanut sauce and cook, stirring, for 2–3 minutes, or until heated through. Tip the mixture into a large serving bowl and allow to cool to room temperature, stirring occasionally. Garnish with the toasted sesame seeds and cucumber julienne strips before serving.

## INGREDIENTS
### Serves 4–8

450 g/1 lb buckwheat (soba) noodles or wholewheat spaghetti
salt
1 tbsp sesame oil
1 tbsp groundnut oil
1 green pepper, deseeded and thinly sliced
125 g/4 oz daikon (mooli), cut into julienne strips
125 g/4 oz mangetout or green beans, trimmed and sliced
2 garlic cloves, peeled and finely chopped
2 tbsp soy sauce, or to taste
1 tbsp cider vinegar
2 tbsp sweet chilli sauce, or to taste
2 tsp sugar
75 g/3 oz peanut butter
6–8 spring onions, trimmed and diagonally sliced

### GARNISH:
toasted sesame seeds
julienne strips of cucumber

## Food Fact

Daikon, also known as mooli or white radish, resembles a parsnip in shape. It has a very fresh, peppery flavour and is often used in salads either peeled or grated. Because it has a high water content, it should be sprinkled with salt and allowed to drain in a sieve over a bowl for about 30 minutes after preparing. Rinse well under cold running water and pat dry on absorbent kitchen paper before stir-frying.

# Singapore Noodles

1 Bring a large pan of lightly salted water to a rolling boil. Add the noodles and cook according to the packet instructions, or until 'al dente'. Drain thoroughly and toss with 1 tablespoon of the oil.

2 Heat the remaining oil in a wok or large frying pan over high heat. Add the mushrooms, ginger, chilli and red pepper and stir-fry for 2 minutes. Add the garlic, courgettes, spring onions and garden peas and stir lightly.

3 Push the vegetables to one side and add the curry paste, tomato ketchup and about 125 ml/4 fl oz hot water. Season to taste with salt or a few drops of soy sauce and allow to boil vigorously, stirring, until the paste is smooth.

4 Stir the reserved egg noodles and the beansprouts into the vegetable mixture and stir-fry until coated with the paste and thoroughly heated through. Season with more soy sauce if necessary, then turn into a large warmed serving bowl or spoon on to individual plates. Garnish with sesame seeds and coriander leaves. Serve immediately.

## Helpful Hint

There is a huge range of curry pastes available, varying from very mild to extremely hot. Obviously, the choice here depends very much on your personal preference, but try to select one with oriental rather than Indian overtones – Thai green or red curry paste would be a good choice.

## INGREDIENTS
### Serves 4

*225 g/8 oz thin round egg noodles*
*3 tbsp groundnut or vegetable oil*
*125 g/4 oz field mushrooms, wiped and thinly sliced*
*2.5 cm/1 inch piece root ginger, peeled and finely chopped*
*1 red chilli, deseeded and thinly sliced*
*1 red pepper, deseeded and thinly sliced*
*2 garlic cloves, peeled and crushed*
*1 medium courgette, cut in half lengthwise and diagonally sliced*
*4-6 spring onions, trimmed and thinly sliced*
*50 g/2 oz frozen garden peas, thawed*
*1 tbsp curry paste*
*2 tbsp tomato ketchup*
*salt or soy sauce*
*125 g/4 oz beansprouts, rinsed and drained*

### TO GARNISH:
*sesame seeds*
*fresh coriander leaves*

# Tortellini, Cherry Tomato & Mozzarella Skewers

1 Preheat the grill and line a grill pan with tinfoil, just before cooking. Bring a large pan of lightly salted water to a rolling boil. Add the tortellini and cook according to the packet instructions, or until 'al dente'. Drain, rinse under cold running water, drain again and toss with 2 tablespoons of the olive oil and reserve.

2 Pour the remaining olive oil into a small bowl. Add the crushed garlic and thyme or basil, then blend well. Season to taste with salt and black pepper and reserve.

3 To assemble the skewers, thread the tortellini alternately with the cherry tomatoes and cubes of mozzarella. Arrange the skewers on the grill pan and brush generously on all sides with the olive oil mixture.

4 Cook the skewers under the preheated grill for about 5 minutes, or until they begin to turn golden, turning them halfway through cooking. Arrange 2 skewers on each plate and garnish with a few basil leaves. Serve immediately with dressed salad leaves.

## INGREDIENTS
*Serves 6*

*250 g/9 oz mixed green and plain cheese or vegetable-filled fresh tortellini*
*150 ml/¼ pint extra virgin olive oil*
*2 garlic cloves, peeled and crushed*
*pinch dried thyme or basil*
*salt and freshly ground black pepper*
*225 g/8 oz cherry tomatoes*
*450 g/1 lb mozzarella, cut into 2.5 cm/1 inch cubes*
*basil leaves, to garnish*
*dressed salad leaves, to serve*

## Helpful Hint

These skewers make an ideal starter for a barbecue. Alternatively, a small quantity of the prepared ingredients can be threaded on to smaller skewers and served as canapés. If using wooden skewers for this recipe, soak them in cold water for at least 30 minutes before cooking to prevent them scorching under the grill. The tips of the skewers may be protected with small pieces of foil.

# Tortellini & Summer Vegetable Salad

1 Bring a large pan of lightly salted water to a rolling boil. Add the tortellini and cook according to the packet instructions, or until 'al dente'.

2 Using a large slotted spoon, transfer the tortellini to a colander to drain. Rinse under cold running water and drain again. Transfer to a large bowl and toss with 2 tablespoons of the olive oil.

3 Return the pasta water to the boil and drop in the green beans and broccoli florets; blanch them for 2 minutes, or until just beginning to soften. Drain, rinse under cold running

water and drain again thoroughly. Add the vegetables to the reserved tortellini.

4 Add the pepper, onion, artichoke hearts, capers and olives to the bowl; stir lightly.

5 Whisk together the vinegar, mustard and brown sugar in a bowl and season to taste with salt and pepper. Slowly whisk in the remaining olive oil to form a thick, creamy dressing. Pour over the tortellini and vegetables, add the chopped basil or parsley and stir until lightly coated. Transfer to a shallow serving dish or salad bowl. Garnish with the hard-boiled egg quarters and serve.

## Food Fact

Black olives are picked when fully ripe and a brownish pink colour and then fermented and oxidised until they become black. Dry-cured black olives can be bought from Italian food shops or the delicatessen counter of some large supermarkets, but if you are unable to get them, use ordinary small black olives instead.

### INGREDIENTS
*Serves 6*

*350 g/12 oz mixed green and plain cheese-filled fresh tortellini*

*150 ml/¼ pint extra virgin olive oil*

*225 g/8 oz fine green beans, trimmed*

*175 g/6 oz broccoli florets*

*1 yellow or red pepper, deseeded and thinly sliced*

*1 red onion, peeled and sliced*

*175 g jar marinated artichoke hearts, drained and halved*

*2 tbsp capers*

*75 g/3 oz dry-cured pitted black olives*

*3 tbsp raspberry or balsamic vinegar*

*1 tbsp Dijon mustard*

*1 tsp soft brown sugar*

*salt and freshly ground black pepper*

*2 tbsp freshly chopped basil or flat-leaf parsley*

*2 quartered hard-boiled eggs, to garnish*

# Fettuccine with Calves' Liver & Calvados

1 Season the flour with the salt, black pepper and paprika, then toss the liver in the flour until well coated.

2 Melt half the butter and 1 tablespoon of the olive oil in a large frying pan and fry the liver in batches for 1 minute, or until just browned but still slightly pink inside. Remove using a slotted spoon and place in a warmed dish.

3 Add the remaining butter to the pan, stir in 1 tablespoon of the seasoned flour and cook for 1 minute. Pour in the Calvados and cider and cook over a high heat for 30 seconds. Stir the cream into the sauce and simmer for 1 minute to thicken slightly, then season to taste. Return the liver to the pan and heat through.

4 Bring a large pan of lightly salted water to a rolling boil. Add the fettuccine and cook according to the packet instructions, about 3–4 minutes, or until 'al dente'.

5 Drain the fettuccine thoroughly, return to the pan and toss in the remaining olive oil. Divide among 4 warmed plates and spoon the liver and sauce over the pasta. Garnish with thyme sprigs and serve immediately.

## Helpful Hint

Calvados is made from apples and adds a fruity taste to this dish, although you can, of course, use ordinary brandy instead. Calves' liver is very tender, with a delicate flavour. It should be cooked over a high heat until the outside is brown and crusty and the centre still slightly pink. Take care not to overcook the liver or you will spoil its taste and texture.

### INGREDIENTS
*Serves 4*

*450 g/1 lb calves' liver, trimmed and thinly sliced*
*50 g/2 oz plain flour*
*salt and freshly ground black pepper*
*1 tsp paprika*
*50 g/2 oz butter*
*1½ tbsp olive oil*
*2 tbsp Calvados*
*150 ml/¼ pint cider*
*150 ml/¼ pint whipping cream*
*350 g/12 oz fresh fettuccine*
*fresh thyme sprigs, to garnish*

# Tagliatelle with Stuffed Pork Escalopes

1 Preheat the oven to 180°C/ 350°F/Gas Mark 4, 10 minutes before cooking. Mix the broccoli with the mozzarella cheese, garlic and beaten eggs. Season to taste with salt and pepper and reserve.

2 Using a meat mallet or rolling pin, pound the escalopes on a sheet of greaseproof paper until 5 mm/¼ inch thick. Divide the broccoli mixture between the escalopes and roll each one up from the shortest side. Place the pork rolls in a lightly oiled oven-proof dish, drizzle over the olive oil and bake in the preheated oven for 40–50 minutes, or until cooked.

3 Meanwhile, melt the butter in a heavy-based pan, stir in the flour and cook for 2 minutes. Remove from the heat and whisk in the milk and stock. Season to taste, stir in the mustard then cook until smooth and thickened. Keep warm.

4 Bring a large pan of lightly salted water to a rolling boil. Add the taglietelle and cook according to the packet instructions, about 3–4 minutes, or until 'al dente'. Drain thoroughly and tip into a warmed serving dish. Slice each pork roll into 3, place on top of the pasta and pour the sauce over. Garnish with sage leaves and serve immediately.

## INGREDIENTS
### Serves 4

150 g/5 oz broccoli florets, finely chopped and blanched

125 g/4 oz mozzarella cheese, grated

1 garlic clove, peeled and crushed

2 large eggs, beaten

salt and freshly ground black pepper

4 thin pork escalopes, weighing about 100 g/3½ oz each

1 tbsp olive oil

25 g/1 oz butter

2 tbsp flour

150 ml/¼ pint milk

150 ml/¼ pint chicken stock

1 tbsp Dijon mustard

225 g/8 oz fresh tagliatelle

sage leaves, to garnish

## Helpful Hint

Pounding the pork escalopes makes them thinner, but tenderises the meat. Brush with a little oil to prevent them sticking to the mallet or rolling pin, or pound (with the blunt side of the mallet) between two sheets of oiled greaseproof paper or clingfilm. Take care not to tear the fibres.

# Spicy Chicken with Open Ravioli & Tomato Sauce

1 Heat the olive oil in a frying pan, add the onion and cook gently for 2–3 minutes then add the cumin, paprika pepper and cinnamon and cook for a further 1 minute. Add the chicken, season to taste with salt and pepper and cook for 3–4 minutes, or until tender. Add the peanut butter and stir until well mixed and reserve.

2 Melt the butter in the frying pan, add the shallot and cook for 2 minutes. Add the tomatoes and garlic and season to taste. Simmer gently for 20 minutes, or until thickened, then keep the sauce warm.

3 Cut each sheet of lasagne into 6 squares. Bring a large pan of lightly salted water to a rolling boil. Add the lasagne squares and cook according to the packet instructions, about 3–4 minutes, or until 'al dente'. Drain the lasagne pieces thoroughly, reserve and keep warm.

4 Layer the pasta squares with the spicy filling on individual warmed plates. Pour over a little of the hot tomato sauce and sprinkle with chopped coriander. Serve immediately.

## INGREDIENTS
*Serves 2–3*

*2 tbsp olive oil*
*1 onion, peeled and finely chopped*
*1 tsp ground cumin*
*1 tsp hot paprika pepper*
*1 tsp ground cinnamon*
*175 g/6 oz boneless and skinless chicken breasts, chopped*
*salt and freshly ground black pepper*
*1 tbsp smooth peanut butter*
*50 g/2 oz butter*
*1 shallot, peeled and finely chopped*
*2 garlic cloves, peeled and crushed*
*400 g can chopped tomatoes*
*125 g/4 oz fresh egg lasagne*
*2 tbsp freshly chopped coriander*

## Helpful Hint

Remember that fresh pasta should be exactly that; buy no more than two days ahead and preferably on the day that you plan to cook it. Because it contains fresh eggs it should always be stored in the refrigerator, kept in its packet or wrapped in non-stick baking parchment, then in clingfilm.

# Farfalle & Chicken in White Wine Sauce

1 Place the chicken breasts between two sheets of greaseproof paper and, using a meat mallet or wooden rolling pin, pound as thinly as possible. Season with salt and pepper and reserve.

2 Mash the feta cheese with a fork and blend with the egg and half the tarragon. Divide the mixture between the chicken breasts and roll up each one. Secure with cocktail sticks.

3 Heat half the butter and all the olive oil in a frying pan, add the onion and cook for 2–3 minutes. Remove, using a slotted spoon, and reserve. Add the chicken parcels to the pan and cook for 3–4 minutes, or until browned.

4 Pour in the wine and the stock and stir in the remaining tarragon. Cover and simmer gently for 10–15 minutes, or until the chicken is cooked.

5 Meanwhile, bring a large pan of lightly salted water to a rolling boil. Add the farfalle and cook according to the packet instructions, about 3–4 minutes, or until 'al dente'. Drain, toss in the remaining butter and tip into a warmed serving dish.

6 Slice each chicken roll into 4 and place on the pasta. Whisk the sauce until smooth, then stir in the soured cream and the reserved onions. Heat the sauce gently, then pour over the chicken. Sprinkle with the parsley and serve immediately.

## Food Fact

Feta is a Greek cheese, traditionally made from ewe's milk, but now more often from cow's milk. It is preserved in brine, which gives it a salty flavour; always drain feta before using.

### INGREDIENTS
*Serves 4*

4 boneless and skinless chicken breasts, about 450 g/1 lb in total weight
salt and freshly ground black pepper
125 g/4 oz feta cheese
1 small egg, beaten
2 tbsp freshly chopped tarragon
50 g/2 oz butter
1 tbsp olive oil
1 onion, peeled and sliced into rings
150 ml/¼ pint white wine
150 ml/¼ pint chicken stock
350 g/12 oz fresh farfalle
3–4 tbsp soured cream
2 tbsp freshly chopped parsley

# Gnocchi Roulade
# with Mozzarella & Spinach

1 Preheat the oven to 240°C/ 475°F/Gas Mark 9, 15 minutes before cooking. Oil and line a large Swiss roll tin (23 cm/9 inch x 33 cm/13 inch) with non-stick baking parchment.

2 Pour the milk into a heavy-based pan and whisk in the semolina. Bring to the boil then simmer, stirring continuously with a wooden spoon, for 3–4 minutes, or until very thick. Remove from heat and stir in the butter and Cheddar cheese until melted. Whisk in the egg yolks and season to taste with salt and pepper. Pour into the lined tin. Cover and allow to cool for 1 hour.

3 Cook the baby spinach in batches in a large pan with 1 teaspoon of water for 3–4 minutes, or until wilted. Drain thoroughly, season to taste with salt, pepper and nutmeg, then allow to cool.

4 Spread the spinach over the cooled semolina mixture and sprinkle over 75 g/3 oz of the mozzarella and half the Parmesan cheese. Bake in the preheated oven for 20 minutes, or until golden.

5 Allow to cool, then roll up like a Swiss roll. Sprinkle with the remaining mozzarella and Parmesan cheese, then bake for another 15–20 minutes, or until golden. Serve immediately with freshly made tomato sauce.

## INGREDIENTS
### Serves 8

600 ml/1 pint milk
125 g/4 oz fine semolina or polenta
25 g/1 oz butter
75 g/3 oz Cheddar cheese, grated
2 medium egg yolks
salt and freshly ground black pepper
700 g/1½ lb baby spinach leaves
½ tsp freshly grated nutmeg
1 garlic clove, peeled and crushed
2 tbsp olive oil
150 g/5 oz mozzarella cheese, grated
2 tbsp freshly grated Parmesan cheese
freshly made tomato sauce, to serve

## Helpful Hint

It is important to use the correct size of tin for this dish, so that the gnocchi mixture is thin enough to roll up. Do not be tempted to put it in the refrigerator to cool or it will become too hard and crack when rolled.

# Penne with Mixed Peppers & Garlic

**1** Preheat the grill and line the grill rack with tinfoil. Cut the peppers in half, deseed and place cut side down on the grill rack. Cook under the grill until the skins become blistered and black all over. Place the peppers in a polythene bag and allow to cool, then discard the skin and slice thinly.

**2** Heat the oil in a heavy-based pan. Add the onion, celery, garlic and bacon and cook for 4–5 minutes, or until the onion has softened. Add the peppers and cook for 1 minute. Pour in the stock and season to taste with salt and pepper. Cover and simmer for 20 minutes.

**3** Meanwhile, bring a large pan of lightly salted water to a rolling boil. Add the penne and cook according to the packet instructions, about 3–4 minutes, or until 'al dente'. Drain thoroughly and return to the pan.

**4** Pour the pepper sauce over the pasta and toss lightly. Tip into a warmed serving dish and sprinkle with the chopped parsley and grated pecorino cheese. Serve immediately with a green salad and warm granary bread.

## INGREDIENTS
### Serves 4

450 g/1 lb green, red and yellow peppers
2 tbsp olive oil
1 large onion, peeled and sliced
1 celery stick, trimmed and finely chopped
2 garlic cloves, peeled and crushed
4 rashers smoked streaky bacon, finely chopped
300 ml/½ pint chicken stock
salt and freshly ground black pepper
350 g/12 oz fresh penne
2 tbsp freshly chopped parsley
2 tbsp pecorino cheese, finely grated

### TO SERVE:
green salad
warm granary bread

## Helpful Hint

Grilling brings out all the delicious flavour of peppers. Do make sure that they are blackened and blistered so that the skins simply slip off. You could also roast the peppers in the oven for this recipe, if preferred. Place them in a roasting tin, brush with a little olive oil and cook at 200°C/400°F/Gas Mark 6 for 25 minutes, or until the skins are slightly charred.

# Spaghetti with Smoked Salmon & Tiger Prawns

**1** Cook the baby spinach leaves in a large pan with 1 teaspoon of water for 3–4 minutes, or until wilted. Drain thoroughly, season to taste with salt, pepper and nutmeg and keep warm. Remove the shells from all but 4 of the tiger prawns and reserve.

**2** Bring a large pan of lightly salted water to a rolling boil. Add the pasta and cook according to the packet instructions, about 3–4 minutes, or until 'al dente'. Drain thoroughly and return to the pan. Stir in the butter and the peeled prawns, cover and keep warm.

**3** Beat the eggs with the dill, season well, then stir into the spaghettini and prawns. Return the pan to the heat briefly, just long enough to lightly scramble the eggs, then remove from the heat. Carefully mix in the smoked salmon strips and the cooked spinach. Toss gently to mix. Tip into a warmed serving dish and garnish with the reserved prawns and dill sprigs. Serve immediately with grated Parmesan cheese.

## INGREDIENTS
*Serves 4*

*225 g/8 oz baby spinach leaves*
*salt and freshly ground black*
*    pepper*
*pinch freshly grated nutmeg*
*225 g/8 oz cooked tiger prawns*
*    in their shells, cooked*
*450 g/1 lb fresh angel hair*
*    spaghetti*
*50 g/2 oz butter*
*3 medium eggs*
*1 tbsp freshly chopped dill, plus*
*    extra to garnish*
*125 g/4 oz smoked salmon, cut*
*    into strips*
*dill sprigs, to garnish*
*2 tbsp grated Parmesan cheese,*
*    to serve*

## Helpful Hint

Make sure that you use cooked and not raw king prawns for this dish. If you buy them raw, remove the heads and shells then briefly sauté in a little olive oil until just pink and opaque. This will take only 3–4 minutes; take care not to overcook them or they will toughen.

# Pasta Ring with Chicken & Sun-dried Tomatoes

1 Preheat the oven to 190°C/ 375°F/Gas Mark 5, 10 minutes before cooking. Lightly brush a 20.5 cm/8 inch ring mould with a little melted butter and dust with the breadcrumbs.

2 Melt 50 g/2 oz of the butter in a heavy-based pan. Add the flour and cook for 1 minute. Whisk in the milk and cook, stirring, until thickened. Add the chopped onion, season to taste with salt and pepper and reserve.

3 Bring a large pan of lightly salted water to a rolling boil. Add the tagliatelle and cook according to the packet instructions, about 3–4 minutes, or until 'al dente'. Drain thoroughly and stir into the white sauce. Pour the pasta mixture into the prepared mould and bake in the preheated oven for 25–30 minutes.

4 Melt the remaining butter in a frying pan, add the chicken and cook for 4–5 minutes, or until cooked. Pour in the wine and cook over a high heat for 30 seconds. Blend the cornflour with 1 teaspoon of water and stir into the pan. Add 1 tablespoon chopped tarragon and the tomatoes. Season well, then cook for a few minutes, until thickened.

5 Allow the pasta to cool for 5 minutes, then unmould on to a large serving plate. Fill the centre with the chicken sauce. Garnish with the remaining tarragon and serve immediately.

## Helpful Hint

To ensure that the pasta turns out easily, brush the ring mould with melted butter, then put in the freezer for 3–4 minutes to harden. Brush again with butter before dusting with the breadcrumbs, making sure it is well-coated.

## INGREDIENTS
*Serves 6*

*125 g/4 oz butter, plus extra for brushing*
*2 tbsp natural white breadcrumbs*
*40 g/1½ oz flour*
*450 ml/¾ pint milk*
*1 small onion, peeled and very finely chopped*
*salt and freshly ground black pepper*
*225 g/8 oz fresh tagliatelle*
*450 g/1 lb chicken breast fillets, skinned and cut into strips*
*200 ml/7 fl oz white wine*
*1 tsp cornflour*
*2 tbsp freshly chopped tarragon*
*2 tbsp chopped sun-dried tomatoes*

# Salmon & Mushroom Linguine

1 Preheat the oven to 190°C/ 375°F/Gas Mark 5, 10 minutes before cooking. Place the salmon in a shallow pan and cover with water. Season well with salt and pepper and bring to the boil, then lower the heat and simmer for 6–8 minutes, or until cooked. Drain and keep warm.

2 Melt 50 g/2 oz of the butter in a heavy-based pan, stir in the flour, cook for 1 minute then whisk in the chicken stock. Simmer gently until thickened. Stir in the cream and season to taste. Keep the sauce warm.

3 Melt the remaining butter, in a pan, add the sliced mushrooms and cook for 2–3 minutes.

Stir the mushrooms into the white sauce.

4 Bring a large pan of lightly salted water to a rolling boil. Add the linguine and cook according to the packet instructions, or until 'al dente'.

5 Drain the pasta thoroughly and return to the pan. Stir in half the sauce, then spoon into a lightly oiled a 1.4 litre/2½ pint shallow ovenproof dish. Flake the salmon, add to the remaining sauce then pour over the pasta. Sprinkle with the cheese and breadcrumbs, then bake in the preheated for 15–20 minutes, or until golden. Garnish with the parsley and serve immediately.

## INGREDIENTS
*Serves 4*

*450 g/1 lb salmon fillets, skinned*
*salt and freshly ground black*
  *pepper*
*75 g/3 oz butter*
*40 g/1½ oz flour*
*300 ml/½ pint chicken stock*
*150 ml/¼ pint whipping cream*
*225 g/8 oz mushrooms, wiped*
  *and sliced*
*350 g/12 oz linguine*
*50 g/2 oz Cheddar cheese, grated*
*50 g/2 oz fresh white*
  *breadcrumbs*
*2 tbsp freshly chopped parsley,*
*to garnish*

## Helpful Hint

When cooking the salmon, the poaching liquid should be just simmering and not boiling rapidly. Add extra flavour if you like by putting in a bay leaf and a sprig of fresh thyme or a thinly pared strip of lemon rind. The salmon should be slightly undercooked in this recipe, as it will then be baked in the oven.

# Spaghetti with Hot Chilli Mussels

1 Scrub the mussels and remove any beards. Discard any that do not close when tapped. Place in a large pan with the white wine and half the crushed garlic. Cover and cook over a high heat for 5–6 minutes, shaking the pan from time to time. When the mussels have opened, drain, reserving the juices and straining them through a muslin-lined sieve. Discard any mussels that have not opened and keep the rest warm.

2 Heat the oil in a heavy-based pan, add the remaining garlic with the chillies and cook for 30 seconds. Stir in the chopped tomatoes and 75 ml/ 3 fl oz of the reserved cooking liquor and simmer for 15–20 minutes. Season to taste with salt and pepper.

3 Meanwhile, bring a large pan of lightly salted water to a rolling boil. Add the spaghetti and cook according to the packet instructions, about 3–4 minutes, or until 'al dente'.

4 Drain the spaghetti thoroughly and return to the pan. Add the mussels and tomato sauce to the pasta, toss lightly to cover, then tip into a warmed serving dish or spoon on to individual plates. Garnish with chopped parsley and serve immediately with warm crusty bread.

## INGREDIENTS
### Serves 4

900 g/2 lb fresh live mussels
300 ml/½ pint white wine
3–4 garlic cloves, peeled and crushed
2 tbsp olive oil
1–2 bird's-eye chillies, deseeded and chopped
2 x 400 g cans chopped tomatoes
salt and freshly ground black pepper
350 g/12 oz fresh spaghetti
2 tbsp freshly chopped parsley, to garnish
warm crusty bread, to serve

## Food Fact

Mussels are bivalves (which means they have two shells hinged together) with blue-black coloured shells. They attach themselves to rocks on the sea-bed and take up to two years to mature. They are usually sold in netted bags, either by weight or volume. If you buy by volume, you will need 1.1 litres/2 pints/1 quart for this recipe.

# Conchiglioni with Crab au Gratin

1 Preheat the oven to 200°C/ 400°F/Gas Mark 6, 15 minutes before cooking. Bring a large pan of lightly salted water to a rolling boil. Add the pasta shells and cook according to the packet instructions, or until 'al dente'. Drain thoroughly and allow to dry completely.

2 Melt half the butter in a heavy-based pan, add the shallots and chilli and cook for 2 minutes, then stir in the crabmeat. Stuff the cooled shells with the crab mixture and reserve.

3 Melt the remaining butter in a small pan and stir in the flour. Cook for 1 minute, then whisk in the wine and milk and cook, stirring, until thickened. Stir in the crème fraîche and grated cheese and season the sauce to taste with salt and pepper.

4 Place the crab filled shells in a lightly oiled, large shallow baking dish or tray and spoon a little of the sauce over. Toss the breadcrumbs in the melted butter or oil, then sprinkle over the pasta shells. Bake in the preheated oven for 10 minutes. Serve immediately with a cheese or tomato sauce and a tossed green salad or cooked baby vegetables.

## Helpful Hint

Canned crabmeat is preserved in brine, so drain well and do not add too much salt when seasoning. Crab is in season between April and December and is least expensive during these months, so consider buying fresh white crabmeat for this recipe; you will need a medium-sized crab which weighs about 350 g/12 oz.

## INGREDIENTS
*Serves 4*

*175 g/6 oz large pasta shells*
*50 g/2 oz butter*
*1 shallot, peeled and finely chopped*
*1 bird's-eye chilli, deseeded and finely chopped*
*2 x 200 g cans crabmeat, drained*
*3 tbsp plain flour*
*50 ml/2 fl oz white wine*
*50 ml/2 fl oz milk*
*3 tbsp crème fraîche*
*15 g/½ oz Cheddar cheese, grated*
*salt and freshly ground black pepper*
*1 tbsp oil or melted butter*
*50 g/2 oz fresh white breadcrumbs*

## TO SERVE:
*cheese or tomato sauce*
*tossed green salad or freshly cooked baby vegetables*

# Pappardelle with Spicy Lamb & Peppers

**1** Preheat the grill just before cooking. Dry fry the minced lamb in a frying pan until browned. Heat the olive oil in a heavy-based pan, add the onion, garlic and all the chopped peppers and cook gently for 3–4 minutes, or until softened. Add the browned lamb mince to the pan and cook stirring, until the onions have softened, then drain off any remaining oil.

**2** Stir the chilli powder and cumin into the pan and cook gently for 2 mintues, stirring frequently. Add the tomato paste, pour in the wine and season to taste with salt and pepper. Reduce the heat and simmer for 10–15 minutes, or until the sauce has reduced.

**3** Meanwhile, bring a large pan of lightly salted water to a rolling boil. Add the papardelle and cook according to the packet instructions, or until 'al dente'. Drain thoroughly, then return to the pan and stir the meat sauce into the pasta. Keep warm.

**4** Meanwhile, place the breadcrumbs on a baking tray, drizzle over the melted butter and place under the pre-heated grill for 3–4 minutes, or until golden and crispy. Allow to cool, then mix with the grated Cheddar cheese. Tip the pasta mixture into a warmed serving dish, sprinkle with the bread-crumbs and the parsley. Serve immediately.

## Tasty Tip

Choose very lean lamb mince for this dish. To add extra flavour, add a fresh bay leaf or a sprig of fresh rosemary to the pan when frying the mince and remove at the end of step 2, when the sauce has reduced.

### INGREDIENTS
*Serves 4*

*450 g/1 lb fresh lamb mince*
*2 tbsp olive oil*
*1 onion, peeled and finely chopped*
*2 garlic cloves, peeled and crushed*
*1 green pepper, deseeded and chopped*
*1 yellow pepper, deseeded and chopped*
*½ tsp hot chilli powder*
*1 tsp ground cumin*
*1 tbsp tomato paste*
*150 ml/¼ pint red wine*
*salt and freshly ground black pepper*
*350 g/12 oz pappardelle*
*2 oz fresh white breadcrumbs*
*25 g/1 oz butter, melted*
*25 g/1 oz Cheddar cheese, grated*
*1 tbsp freshly chopped parsley*

# Farfalle with Courgettes & Mushrooms

**1** Heat the butter and olive oil in a large pan, add the onion, garlic and bacon lardons and cook for 3–4 minutes, or until the onion has softened. Add the courgettes and cook, stirring, for 3–4 minutes. Add the mushrooms, lower the heat and cook, covered, for 4–5 minutes.

**2** Meanwhile, bring a large pan of lightly salted water to a rolling boil. Add the fusilli and cook according to the packet instructions, or until 'al dente'. Drain thoroughly, return to the pan and keep warm.

**3** Season the mushroom mixture to taste with salt and pepper, then stir in the crème fraîche and half the chopped parsley. Simmer for 2–3 minutes, or until the sauce is thick and creamy.

**4** Pour the sauce over the cooked pasta, toss lightly, then reheat for 2 minutes, or until piping hot. Tip into a warmed serving dish and sprinkle over the chopped parsley. Garnish with pecorino cheese shavings and serve immediately with a mixed salad and crusty bread.

## Helpful Hint

To shave pecorino or Parmesan cheese, use a sharp knife or a vegetable peeler. If you find this difficult, you could coarsely grate the cheese instead. Avoid tubs of ready-grated pecorino and Parmesan; they tend to be powdery and flavourless and are a poor substitute for fresh cheese.

---

### INGREDIENTS
*Serves 4*

*25 g/1 oz butter*
*2 tsp olive oil*
*1 small onion, peeled and finely chopped*
*2 garlic cloves, peeled and crushed*
*125 g/4 oz bacon lardons*
*450 g/1 lb courgettes, trimmed and diced*
*125 g/4 oz button mushrooms, wiped and roughly chopped*
*350 g/12 oz farfalle*
*salt and freshly ground black pepper*
*250 ml carton crème fraîche*
*2 tbsp freshly chopped parsley*
*shaved pecorino cheese, to garnish*

*TO SERVE:*
*mixed salad*
*crusty bread*

# Cannelloni with Tomato & Red Wine Sauce

**1** Preheat the oven to 200°C/ 400°F/Gas Mark 6, 15 minutes before cooking. Heat the oil in a heavy-based pan, add the onion and garlic and cook for 2–3 minutes. Cool slightly, then stir in the ricotta cheese and pine nuts. Season the filling to taste with salt, pepper and the nutmeg.

**2** Cut each lasagne sheet in half, put a little of the ricotta filling on each piece and roll up like a cigar to resemble cannelloni tubes. Arrange the cannelloni, seam-side down, in a single layer, in a lightly oiled, 2.3 litre/4 pint shallow ovenproof dish.

**3** Melt the butter in a pan, add the shallot and cook for 2 minutes. Pour in the red wine, tomatoes and sugar and season well. Bring to the boil, lower the heat and simmer for about 20 minutes, or until thickened. Add a little more sugar if desired. Transfer to a food processor and blend until a smooth sauce is formed.

**4** Pour the warm tomato sauce over the cannelloni and sprinkle with the grated mozzarella cheese. Bake in the preheated oven for about 30 minutes, or until golden and bubbling. Garnish and serve immediately with a green salad.

## Food Fact

Mozzarella is the Italian cheese often used to top pizzas, as it is elastic and stringy when cooked. It is a soft, kneaded, brilliantly white cheese with a delicate, almost spongy texture. Traditionally, it was made from buffalo milk, but now cow's milk is used more often.

### INGREDIENTS
*Serves 6*

2 tbsp olive oil
1 onion, peeled and finely
  chopped
1 garlic clove, peeled and crushed
250 g carton ricotta cheese
50 g/2 oz pine nuts
salt and freshly ground black
  pepper
pinch freshly grated nutmeg
250 g/9 oz fresh spinach lasagne
25 g/1 oz butter
1 shallot, peeled and finely
  chopped
150 ml/¼ pint red wine
400 g can chopped tomatoes
½ tsp sugar
50 g/2 oz mozzarella cheese,
  grated, plus extra to serve
1 tbsp freshly chopped parsley, to
  garnish
fresh green salad, to serve

# Pasta Triangles with Pesto & Walnut Dressing

**1** Preheat the grill to high. Cut the lasagne sheets in half, then into triangles and reserve. Mix the pesto and ricotta cheese together and warm gently in a pan.

**2** Toast the walnuts under the preheated grill until golden. Rub off the papery skins. Place the nuts in a food processor with the bread and grind finely.

**3** Mix the soured cream with the mascarpone cheese in a bowl. Add the ground walnuts and grated pecorino cheese and season to taste with salt and pepper. Whisk in the olive oil. Pour into a pan and warm gently.

**4** Bring a large pan of lightly salted water to a rolling boil. Add the pasta triangles and cook, according to the packet instructions, about 3–4 minutes, or until 'al dente'.

**5** Drain the pasta thoroughly and arrange a few triangles on each serving plate. Top each one with a spoonful of the pesto mixture then place another triangle on top. Continue to layer the pasta and pesto mixture, then spoon a little of the walnut sauce on top of each stack. Garnish with dill, basil or parsley and serve immediately with a freshly dressed tomato and cucumber salad.

## INGREDIENTS
### Serves 6

450 g/1 lb fresh egg lasagne
4 tbsp ricotta cheese
4 tbsp pesto
125 g/4 oz walnuts
1 slice white bread, crusts removed
150 ml/¼ pint soured cream
75 g/3 oz mascarpone cheese
25 g/1 oz pecorino cheese, grated
salt and freshly ground black
 pepper
1 tbsp olive oil
sprig of dill or freshly chopped
 basil or parsley, to garnish
tomato and cucumber salad,
 to serve

## Tasty Tip

For a simple tomato and cucumber salad, arrange overlapping thin slices of cucumber and beef and plum tomatoes on a large plate. Drizzle over a dressing made with 1 teaspoon Dijon mustard, 4 tablespoons extra virgin olive oil, 1 tablespoon lemon juice and a pinch each of caster sugar, salt and pepper. Leave at room temperature for 15 minutes before serving.

# Aubergine & Tomato Layer

1 Preheat the oven to 190°C/375°F/Gas Mark 5, 10 minutes before cooking. Brush the aubergine slices with 5 tablespoons of the olive oil and place on a baking sheet. Bake in the preheated oven for 20 minutes, or until tender. Remove from the oven and increase the temperature to 200°C/400°F/Gas Mark 6.

2 Heat the remaining oil in a heavy-based pan. Add the onion and garlic, cook for 2–3 minutes then add the tomatoes, wine and sugar. Season to taste with salt and pepper, then simmer for 20 minutes.

3 Melt the butter in another pan. Stir in the flour, cook for 2 minutes, then whisk in the milk. Cook for 2–3 minutes, or until thickened. Season to taste.

4 Pour a little white sauce into a lightly oiled, 1.7 litre/3 pint baking dish. Cover with a layer of lasagne, spread with tomato sauce, then add some of the aubergines. Cover thinly with white sauce and sprinkle with a little cheese. Continue to layer in this way, finishing with a layer of lasagne.

5 Beat together the eggs and yogurt. Season, then pour over the lasagne. Sprinkle with the remaining cheese and bake in the preheated oven for 25–30 minutes, or until golden. Garnish with basil leaves and serve.

## INGREDIENTS
### Serves 4

2 aubergines, about 700 g/1½ lb, trimmed and thinly sliced
6 tbsp olive oil
1 onion, peeled and finely sliced
1 garlic clove, peeled and crushed
400 g can chopped tomatoes
50 ml/2 fl oz red wine
½ tsp sugar
salt and freshly ground black pepper
50 g/2 oz butter
40 g/1½ oz flour
450 ml/¾ pint milk
225 g/8 oz fresh egg lasagne
2 medium eggs, beaten
200 ml/7 fl oz Greek yogurt
125 g/3 oz mozzarella cheese, grated
fresh basil leaves, to garnish

## Food Fact

Greek yogurt can be made from either ewe's or cow's milk. Ewes milk is very rich and creamy, with a fat content of around 6 per cent. Cow's milk has less fat, so the yogurt is strained to concentrate it.

# Cannelloni with Gorgonzola Sauce

1 Preheat the oven to 190°C/ 375°F/Gas Mark 5, 10 minutes before cooking. Melt the salted butter in a heavy-based pan, add the shallot and bacon and cook for about 4–5 minutes.

2 Add the mushrooms to the pan and cook for 5–6 minutes, or until the mushrooms are very soft. Stir in the flour, cook for 1 minute, then stir in the double cream and cook gently for 2 minutes. Allow to cool.

3 Cut each sheet of lasagne in half. Spoon some filling on to each piece and roll up from the longest side to resemble cannelloni. Arrange the cannelloni in a lightly oiled, shallow 1.4 litre/2½ pint ovenproof dish.

4 Heat the unsalted butter very slowly in a pan and when melted, add the Gorgonzola cheese. Stir until the cheese has melted, then stir in the whipping cream. Bring to the boil slowly, then simmer gently for about 5 minutes, or until thickened.

5 Pour the cream sauce over the cannelloni. Place in the preheated oven and bake for 20 minutes, or until golden and thoroughly heated through. Serve immediately with assorted salad leaves.

## INGREDIENTS
### Serves 2–3

50 g/2 oz salted butter
1 shallot, peeled and finely chopped
2 rashers streaky bacon, rind removed and chopped
225 g/8 oz mushrooms, wiped and finely chopped
25 g/1 oz plain flour
120 ml/4 fl oz double cream
125 g/4 oz fresh egg lasagne, 6 sheets in total
40 g/1½ oz unsalted butter
150 g/5 oz Gorgonzola cheese, diced
150 ml/¼ pint whipping cream
assorted salad leaves, to serve

## Tasty Tip

Gorgonzola cheese is very salty. As it is combined in this recipe with bacon, which is also salty, some of the butter used here is unsalted in order to balance the flavour. Italians use a wide range of mushrooms in their cooking, so for extra taste, you could use chestnut or large open field mushrooms instead of ordinary button mushrooms.

# Ratatouille & Pasta Bake

1 Preheat the oven to 190°C/ 375°F/Gas Mark 5, 10 minutes before cooking. Heat the olive oil in a heavy-based pan, add half the onion and cook gently for 2–3 minutes. Stir in the tomatoes and wine, then simmer for 20 minutes, or until a thick consistency is formed. Add the sugar and season to taste with salt and pepper. Reserve.

2 Meanwhile, melt the butter in another pan, add the remaining onion, the garlic, mushrooms and courgettes and cook for 10 minutes, or until softened.

3 Spread a little tomato sauce in the base of a lightly oiled, 1.4 litre/2 ½ pint baking dish. Top with a layer of lasagne and spoon over half the mushroom and courgette mixture. Repeat the layers, finishing with a layer of lasagne.

4 Beat the eggs and cream together, then pour over the lasagne. Mix the mozzarella and pecorino cheeses together then sprinkle on top of the lasagne. Place in the preheated oven and cook for 20 minutes, or until golden-brown. Serve immediately with a green salad.

## INGREDIENTS
### Serves 4

1 tbsp olive oil
2 large onions, peeled and finely chopped
400 g can chopped tomatoes
100 ml/3½ fl oz white wine
½ tsp caster sugar
salt and freshly ground black pepper
40 g/1½ oz butter
2 garlic cloves, peeled and crushed
125 g/4 oz mushrooms, wiped and thickly sliced
700 g/1½ lb courgettes, trimmed and thickly sliced
125 g/4 oz fresh spinach lasagne
2 large eggs
2 tbsp double cream
75 g/3 oz mozzarella cheese, grated
25 g/1 oz pecorino cheese, grated
green salad, to serve

## Tasty Tip

For speed and simplicity, this recipe is a simplified version of ratatouille. If preferred, it can be made more traditionally by substituting a small chopped aubergine and a deseeded and chopped green or red pepper for some of the courgettes.

# Lamb & Pasta Pie

1 Preheat the oven to 190° C/ 375°F/Gas Mark 5, 10 minutes before cooking. Lightly oil a 20.5 cm/8 inch spring-form cake tin. Blend the flour, salt, margarine and white vegetable fat in a food processor and add sufficient cold water to make a smooth, pliable dough. Knead on a lightly floured surface, then roll out two-thirds to line the base and sides of the tin. Brush the pastry with egg white and reserve.

2 Melt the butter in a heavy-based pan, stir in the flour and cook for 2 minutes. Stir in the milk and cook, stirring, until a smooth, thick sauce is formed. Season to taste with salt and pepper and reserve.

3 Bring a large pan of lightly salted water to a rolling boil. Add the macaroni and cook according to the packet instructions, or until 'al dente'.

Drain, then stir into the white sauce with the grated cheese.

4 Heat the oil in a frying pan, add the onion, garlic, celery and lamb mince and cook, stirring, for 5–6 minutes. Stir in the tomato paste and tomatoes and cook for 10 minutes. Cool slightly.

5 Place half the pasta mixture, then all the mince in the pastry-lined tin. Top with a layer of pasta. Roll out the remaining pastry and cut out a lid. Brush the edge with water, place over the filling and pinch the edges together. Use trimmings to decorate the top of the pie.

6 Brush the pie with beaten egg yolk and bake in the preheated oven for 50–60 minutes, covering the top with tin- foil if browning too quickly. Stand for 15 minutes before turning out. Serve immediately.

## INGREDIENTS
*Serves 8*

400 g/14 oz plain white flour
100 g/3½ oz margarine
100 g/3½ oz white vegetable fat
pinch of salt
1 small egg, separated
50 g/2 oz butter
50 g/2 oz flour
450 ml/¾ pint milk
salt and freshly ground black
    pepper
225 g/8 oz macaroni
50 g/2 oz Cheddar cheese, grated
1 tbsp vegetable oil
1 onion, peeled and chopped
1 garlic clove, peeled and crushed
2 celery sticks, trimmed and
    chopped
450 g/1 lb lamb mince
1 tbsp tomato paste
400 g can chopped tomatoes

# Baked Macaroni with Mushrooms & Leeks

**1** Preheat the oven to 220°C/ 425° F/Gas Mark 7, 15 minutes before cooking. Heat 1 tablespoon of the olive oil in a large frying pan, add the onion and garlic and cook for 2 minutes. Add the leeks, mushrooms and 25 g/1 oz of the butter then cook for 5 minutes. Pour in the white wine, cook for 2 minutes then stir in the crème fraîche or cream. Season to taste with salt and pepper.

**2** Meanwhile, bring a large pan of lightly salted water to a rolling boil. Add the macaroni and cook according to the packet instructions, or until 'al dente'.

**3** Melt 25 g/1 oz of the butter with the remaining oil in a small frying pan. Add the breadcrumbs and fry until just beginning to turn golden-brown. Drain on absorbent kitchen paper.

**4** Drain the pasta thoroughly, toss in the remaining butter then tip into a lightly oiled, 1.4 litre/2½ pint shallow baking dish. Cover the pasta with the leek and mushroom mixture then sprinkle with the fried breadcrumbs. Bake in the preheated oven for 5–10 minutes, or until golden and crisp. Garnish with chopped parsley and serve.

## INGREDIENTS
### Serves 4

2 tbsp olive oil

1 onion, peeled and finely chopped

1 garlic clove, peeled and crushed

2 small leeks, trimmed and chopped

450 g/1 lb assorted wild mushrooms, trimmed

50 ml/2 fl oz white wine

75 g/3 oz butter

150 ml/¼ pint crème fraîche or whipping cream

salt and freshly ground black pepper

75 g/3 oz fresh white breadcrumbs

350 g/12 oz short cut macaroni

1 tbsp freshly chopped parsley, to garnish

## Helpful Hint

Some wild mushrooms are more tender and cook faster than others. Chestnut, porcini (ceps), portabello, enoki and shiitake would all be good used here. If you use chanterelles or oyster mushrooms, sauté them with the leeks for 1 minute only as they are fairly delicate.

# INDEX